FROM SCATTERED ASHES

by
Mark Garnett

Cover art by Jordan Murdock-Thompson

Contents

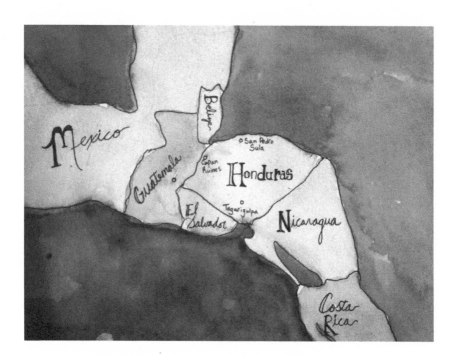

The following story is true. It happened during
the months of January and June in the year 2014.
Most of the names of the people and places
have been changed, but not at the expense of the story.

This book is for the bad Christians.
You know who you are:
you who want so desperately to believe,
but wonder most days why it seems to come
so easily for everyone in the world but you.
You, my friends, are the reason I wrote this book.

You are not crazy.
You are not worthless.
You are not alone.

PART ONE

rediscovering

Chapter 1

Genesis

Bvvvrt-bvvvvvvvrt

bvvvrt-bvvvvvvvrt

BVVVRT-BVVVRT-BVVVVVVVVRT

Ignoring the alarm that morning wasn't an option. It was the day I'd been waiting for since September. Tempting though it was to simply roll over and fall back into unconsciousness, I knew there wasn't time. If I didn't get up now, Mom and Dad would wake me up in twenty or thirty minutes, and I'd have to skip a shower. This day was going to be long, and a shower wasn't a sacrifice I was willing to make. Still, after only two hours of sleep, repeatedly interrupted by violent coughing, nothing felt as precious as those few extra seconds in bed with my eyelids closed.

Get up, I told myself, forcing my eyes open and blinking them into focus. The rhythmic vibration of my cell phone sounded like a parade of elephants against the wooden nightstand. I heaved one arm over my body and yanked the phone from its charger. In a blaze of blinding light, the screen confirmed the alarm's announcement:

January 2.

2:30 a.m.

I had a flight to catch.

The room went dark as I disabled the alarm, but seconds later, the thin crack in the doorframe was highlighted by warm light from the hallway. Dad's shadow quickly passed by the door, followed by Mom's. Soon, the fresh scent of coffee seeped through the crack, accompanied by soft murmuring from the kitchen.

This is really happening.

Get up.

Now.

Throwing the blanket from the bed, I bolted upright and let out an excruciating cough. I was fed up with being sick. I'd spent the last week in a battle of wills against a cold that refused to let up. It was nothing serious—a cough mostly, but one hell-bent on making the last few days miserable.

Dragging myself to the bathroom took every ounce of willpower I had, but the shower that followed did wonders: I emerged fully awake and ready to take on the day. I covered my lower half with a towel and darted across the hall, pulling the bedroom door closed behind me.

Beside the bed sat the wadded pair of blue jeans I'd worn less than three hours ago. Operating on such little sleep was commonplace; mere weeks had passed since finals week at college. And anyway, the airport wouldn't care how tired I was. My plane would take off at 6:00 a.m. whether I was ready or not.

Stretching a t-shirt over my wet, fuzzy hair, I flipped the light switch and left the bedroom. Taylor stood at the end of the hall, rubbing her eyes. She must have just woken up. Her hands fell to her side and our eyes met. Even on three hours of sleep, she was stunning. Walking the length of the hall, I took her into my arms and held tightly.

I was in love.

"Good morning, beautiful," I whispered through her curly, red hair with my terrible morning breath. She mumbled a few words into my chest, muffled beyond recognition. We walked to the living room, hand in hand, and stood over the two purple bags on the floor, stuffed and zipped tight. Over the last week, Taylor had lent me her packing expertise. I decided what would stay or go, then passed it to Taylor, who folded it and packed it away. Together, we'd driven three hours north to my parents' house in Kansas City, where we stayed overnight to say our goodbyes at the airport the following morning.

Taylor and I had a lot in common. We had the same sense of humor, the same genuine love of people, and more than anything else, the same passion to see the world; it was what brought us together in the first place. Adventure was the heartbeat of our relationship. More often than not, though, the "adventures" of two college students working in a mall food court consisted of walking through parks, trying new

4

restaurants, and watching old movies. Still, if we did it together, it was enough.

I hadn't realized how cold it was that January morning until I opened the garage and allowed a gust of frigid air inside, stinging my exposed toes. Flip-flops probably weren't the ideal choice for travel, but since my tennis shoes were packed away, they would have to do. Walking down the snow-laden driveway, Taylor and I threw the bags into the minivan parked on the curbside. She wasted no time running back to the house as soon as the case left her hands. I took my time at first, but the bite of the wind soon had me scampering too.

Mom and Dad left the radio off as we drove to the airport. The silence brought with it a peace, echoed by the stillness of the sleeping city covered in a fresh blanket of snow. I spent most of the drive peering out the windows, reminding myself that I wouldn't see these familiar sights for months. In the distance, a digital bank sign flashed the time and temperature in warm, red numbers:

3:52 a.m.

-2°F

My hand clasped Taylor's tightly as a flood of feelings and thoughts fought for my attention. How could I be so excited and so worried at the same time?

"You're going to love it," Taylor had assured me just before Christmas.

"Probably," I agreed. "Still, six months without my friends, my church, without *you*—it won't be easy."

Taylor looked at me with her soft, blue eyes, gently illuminated by the glow of the Christmas tree. "I've got something to help with that," she said, passing me a small box wrapped in bright red paper. "I made this for you—for whenever you're lonely or you need a pick-me-up."

Inside the box was a black USB drive. "What's this?" I asked, holding it between my thumb and index finger.

"*This* is so you don't forget about me and decide to stay in Honduras," she said with a grin. "I filled it with a bunch of pictures and notes, and I recorded a few videos. You know—just encouragement."

I was speechless. It was the best Christmas gift I could have received. "I love you," I told her, caressing her cheek with my thumb.

"I love *you*," she smiled back, offering a kiss to confirm it. "Merry Christmas, Mark."

That night played in my mind like a scene from a movie as I stared out the window of the minivan. Leaving Taylor would be harder than I had prepared for. In that moment, I considered calling the whole thing off, demanding that Dad turn the van around and go back home. It would have been all too easy to give in to the fear of uncertainty that so plagued my mind.

It wasn't like I was apprehensive about all of it. This had been my choice and I was riding a wave of excitement. I was the one who had made all the preparations over the last four months. It had been my idea in the first place. Still, I could no longer ignore the building fear—the fear of failure, of loneliness, of finding out things about myself that I hoped weren't true. What if I wasn't cut out for this?

What am I getting myself into?

The thought had barely finished before the final exit sign for Kansas City International Airport zipped by. This was certainly the beginning of a dream come true. I only hoped that it wouldn't turn out to be a nightmare.

I'd spent hours praying about it, probably more than anything else I've ever prayed about in my life. As a kid, I was taught that prayer was the most important factor in making big decisions.

Well, this might have been the biggest decision I had ever made.

I'd been a Christian for as long as I could remember. Mom and Dad got heavily involved in a Southern Baptist church when I was five, and they are still there to this day. If the doors were unlocked, we were there. By age eight, I could recite all sixty-six books of the Bible in order. At eleven, I could quote just about any verse in the Awana handbook. And by sixteen, I could explain how the Great Flood in Genesis killed all the dinosaurs, which of course, coexisted right alongside humans. I knew it all, and it felt good.

I spent the first twenty years of my life with my parents in

Kansas City. Around the time I graduated high school, I got the itch to move out, to live on my own, to be an adult. Through a series of risks and mishaps, I eventually landed in Joplin—a town in southwest Missouri that no one had ever heard of before 2011, when a giant tornado ripped it in half. The move was everything I hoped for and far more. I joined a church, made a million friends, and even decided to finish college.

In the Spring of 2012, I enrolled at Ozark Christian College. A lot of OCC students will tell you that, after months of prayer and wise counsel, they felt God's specific calling to Ozark; I chose the school because I didn't want to take math classes.

A couple semesters in, one particular major caught my eye: TESOL, or "Teaching English to Speakers of Other Languages". Being a fanatic for traveling the world and meeting people from different cultures, I declared TESOL as my major and dreamed of the day when I would put my education to use somewhere in the big blue world.

That opportunity came in an endlessly forwarded email during my final semester at OCC. Attached was a flyer, offering a paid teaching position at a small private school in Honduras. At the time, I didn't even know where Honduras was (somewhere in Africa, right?), but I leaped at the opportunity. Two emails and a few legal documents later, I was formally offered a six-month paid teaching position at Santa Lucia Bilingual School in Oranado, Honduras.

I was ecstatic at the chance to fulfill my lifelong dream of traveling; the one thing I'd strived for over the last three years—at the age of 25, no less. Never mind that Honduras was a third world country or that I didn't know a word of Spanish. This was an opportunity that I might never have again. The question was not whether I would accept the offer, but how soon I could begin.

Taylor supported me, my parents supported me, my friends and church supported me, and I was certain that God supported me. All the pieces had fallen into place. One final semester of college was all that stood between me and my Great Honduran Adventure.

That final semester, though, was different than the others. Until that point, I had taken the majority of my classes at OCC. I decided, for the sake of time and money, to take a certain class through the local State

University, Missouri Southern. That class was Anthropology 101.

Anthropology is the study of humankind, including society, language, ecology, and evolution. That last one is somewhat of a buzzword in those parts of the United States. A lot of Bible Belt preachers stay away from "the E-word," except in sermons about Genesis 1, where the Bible *clearly* states that the earth and everything in it was created whole and complete. Until that point in my life, I hadn't faced the hard facts of science, and was quite content to ignore the evidence against a literal six-day creation story. I was hesitant to publicly argue the point, but I was comfortable disregarding godless evolution myths in my own mind.

Anthropology 101 made that blissful ignorance impossible.

I don't know what Anthropology would have been like at Ozark Christian College, but it must have been radically different from the class I took at MSSU. The hardest part of going to class and learning contradictory information to what I believed about the Bible was that most of it made sense. One by one, the foundational building blocks of my faith-based Jenga tower were plucked out, until the tower became dangerously unstable.

It was at this point that I began to realize how many aspects of my life were tied to each other; you simply can't pull the strings of one area without tugging at the whole. Praying was always hard for me, but when I began questioning the foundations of my faith, I stopped trying to pray altogether. I read the Bible scarcely, but even then, I didn't hold it in any sort of esteem. I believed in a god, but I wasn't sure which one or what it was exactly that I believed about him, or her, or them. By the time I graduated in December, my faith had all but disappeared. God was little more than an afterthought.

Even amidst the doubts and questions, I decided to go ahead with my plans. Honduras was waiting for me, and I wasn't about to let *anything* get in the way of my next adventure. Still, there was no denying that for the first time in my life, I didn't know what I believed.

Chapter 2

Honduras

There are few places I love more than the airport. Sometimes I go simply to watch people arrive and set out to far-away destinations. I scan the arrival times and wonder what sort of business someone might've had in Japan or Israel. I love watching planes leave the ground and soar high above the clouds. A sense of adventure lingers over the terminals as hundreds of travelers prepare to board planes and reemerge into a completely different country and culture.

The vibe was no different that morning; Mom, Dad, Taylor, and I meandered aimlessly through KCI. They took pictures while I checked my bags at the front counter. We spent the remaining few minutes in conversation, just outside the gate. Whether intentionally or not, no one mentioned the days to come. The conversation gradually tapered off until, at last, there was nothing left to be said. Dad's eyes glanced to the departure times, then back to me. He didn't say it; he didn't have to. It was time.

We all hugged. Mom told me to be careful. I locked Taylor tightly in my arms, knowing that I wouldn't have this luxury again for six long months.

"I love you," I whispered into her ear.

She took my cheeks in her warm hands and looked into my eyes. "I love you, too," she said, pulling my face in for a quick kiss. Then she smiled and said, "Now go get on that plane."

I tugged the straps on my backpack, ensuring it was firm on my shoulders, then walked to the gate and scanned my ticket. Catching one last glimpse of my parents and the girl I loved, I waved a final time, then took a seat in the crowded waiting area. Ten minutes later, I boarded the plane.

Finding my seat and slithering past the man shoving his bag into the overhead compartment, I plopped down and made myself comfortable. The window shade was wide open; a sure omen of a great view to come. *This is going to be good*, I assured myself, and for the first time in weeks, I believed it.

Takeoff was delayed because of ice. By the time we left the ground, we were forty minutes behind schedule. This meant that my already-slim window to catch my connecting flight was squeezed even tighter.

When we landed in Atlanta, I sprinted across three terminals, arriving at my connecting flight with only nine minutes to spare (a new personal record). Of course, all the gasping for air didn't help my cough. When I boarded the plane, I looked and sounded like a giant red gummy bear spouting out gorilla mating calls.

It was a bit surreal to hear so much Spanish around the cabin— my first concrete indication that I was actually on my way to Central America. There was no going back now. Soon after takeoff, a digital map appeared on the screen near the front of the cabin. It stretched from Colorado to Costa Rica, with a dotted line connecting Georgia and Honduras. I was surprised; Central America had seemed so far before. Now it seemed only a hop, skip, and jump over the Gulf of Mexico.

In three hours, we'd nearly reached our destination. As the plane made a sharp turn to the left, the young boy two seats away lifted the window shade with all his might, and a burst of sunlight exploded into the cabin. I leaned my head inward to get a peek at the ocean below, surprised instead to see land in every direction. We were very close now. Not a minute later, a voice came over the intercom, first in Spanish, then in English:

"*Señoras y señores, estamos empezando el descenso final hacia San Pedro Sula.* Ladies and gentlemen, we are now beginning our final descent into San Pedro Sula."

The plane descended through a cloudless sky and landed comfortably on the soft runway. Far in the distance, the earth was covered in lush, green mountains. Peeling my sweaty back from the leather seat for the first time in three hours, I reached my arms high above my head and stretched them out. The mother of the young boy reached out and tapped my shoulder. She smiled. "I hope your cold gets better," she said with a thick Spanish accent.

"Gracias," I offered, cutting myself short before trying any more Spanish.

The line of passengers moved slowly from the plane, as the tropical heat seeped through the cracks of the jet bridge and sadistically welcomed us to the tropics. It was 98°F that day in San Pedro Sula. In less than six hours, I had experienced a temperature change of almost one hundred degrees.

I followed the foot traffic, filing through the long hallway lined with floor-to-ceiling windows. The hall led to an escalator that would take us downstairs to Customs. Half way down, a sign hung from the ceiling:

¡Bienvenidos a Honduras!
Welcome to Honduras!

Thanks, Honduras, I thought. *It's nice to be here, at last.*

Foot traffic was funneled through a doorway just past customs. The airport opened to a giant terminal, full of restaurants and gift shops. A glass wall on the far side bathed the terminal in warm sunlight.

"Mark!" I heard a female voice shout from my right. My head darted to the side, catching a vaguely familiar face in the crowd. Her smile was wide and bright as she waved her hand over the throng. Nudging my body through the sea of travelers, I made my way to her outstretched arm.

Hissela Hidalga Alvarez was my only Honduran contact. She was the founder and principal of Santa Lucia Bilingual School. I'd video chatted with her once in the months leading up to the trip. My only visual frame of reference was what I could remember from that short, grainy conversation nearly three months ago. Fortunately, as soon as I stepped into the main terminal, she recognized me.

"How are you?" she asked in a delightful Spanish accent.

I began to answer, but was overwhelmed with a fit of coughing. Any answer surely would have been lost in the chaos anyway.

We quickly moved out of the crowd. Hissela was accompanied by her nephew, Jorge, who spoke English fluently with hardly a trace of an accent. After brief introductions, Jorge took my bags, and we followed Hissela through the exit doors. The sun's rays landed hard on the blacktop of the parking lot, searing all who dared to cross. I stripped off my yellow jacket and used it to wipe the sweat from my forehead. Hissela told us to wait on the curb while she got the Jeep.

In a few minutes, the bags were nestled safely in the back, and we were on our way. Jorge offered me the front seat, giving Hissela an opportunity for another attempt at conversation.

"How was your flight?" she asked.

"Not bad," I answered. "I like really like to fl..." I cut myself short, desperately trying to repress another cough.

Riding shotgun gave me a chance to get a good look at Hissela. She was older than I had guessed over the computer; she couldn't have been younger than fifty. Her face, while not wrinkled, was weathered, and told the story of a full life. Thick, black hair fell freely just above her collar. The reflection of her glasses hid her deep, brown eyes, but when she smiled (and she seemed to always be smiling), a twinkle shown through. She had no trouble keeping a conversation in English, though her heavy accent gave her away.

Staring through the dusty windshield, I was struck by how similar Honduras looked to any given U.S. city—although perhaps a bit more rustic and worn down. The busy urban streets were lined with KFC, McDonald's, Pizza Hut, and various, unmarked buildings. There were billboards and dumpsters at every corner. The only major contrast was the lack of anything green.

As we drove deeper into the bustling city, though, I began to notice subtle differences: bright, painted concrete walls surrounded the homes and shops, enormous groups of pedestrians filled the sidewalks and roads, giant speakers rested against the walls of gas stations, polluting the air with the sound of thumping bass lines, and of course, everything was written in Spanish.

My short tour of San Pedro Sula also came with strict instructions: "Do not roll down your window or make eye contact when we stop." Before long, I began to understand why. Police with shotguns patrolled the streets at every corner while razor wire and glass shards stood guard atop the walls and fences. Thick, steel bars guarded any and

12

all exposed glass on the buildings. San Pedro Sula hadn't earned the title of "most dangerous city on earth" for nothing.

"Honduras boasts the highest murder rate per capita in the world." This fact had been drilled into my head during the months leading up to my trip. At first, I shrugged it off. Over time, though, it began to command more and more attention, until finally, it earned its place in my stack of growing fears. Now, seeing the reality of how dangerous Honduras really was brought that fear to the forefront of my mind.

How do people live like this? I wondered, as we passed a group of men in torn jeans and paisley bandanas. Each one held a cigarette between his lips, and not a one looked liked he wouldn't kill me if given the chance. *How do these people live in a place so ripe with danger?* And then another thought hit me: *How am I going to survive down here until June?*

"Are you hungry?" Hissela asked, yanking me from my trance.

"S-sure," I said, pulling my face from the window. "I could eat." It would be my first exposure to Honduran food. Nervous though I was, I knew it had to come sooner or later.

"I'm sure I'll like it," I had told a handful of friends in Missouri. "I could eat Mexican food every day of my life." Later that day, I was pulled aside and scolded for my ignorance. "Mexico and Honduras are two separate countries with *completely* different cultures," I was told. "And you'd be a fool to think you understand one based on the other." It stung at the time, but it was a lesson I'm glad to have learned sooner rather than later.

The Jeep pulled into the parking lot of a fast food restaurant. A sign with the words *Mighty Pollo* over an enormous muscular chicken stood tall above the entrance. Inside, a crowd pressed against the front counter. It was first-come-first-served. Hissela told Jorge and me to find a seat while she ordered. We walked to the back of the restaurant to what I presumed was once an indoor playground, now filled with benches and tables.

"Let's sit here," Jorge said, tapping his fingers on a clean table near the wall. "I am going to use the restroom. Will you be ok for a few minutes?"

13

I nodded. "Yeah, I'll be fine."

I took a seat as he disappeared behind the crowd. Leaning to my left, I reached into my pocket to retrieve my cell phone, but came back empty handed. Of course I hadn't brought my cellphone to Honduras. What an adjustment this was going to be.

I leaned back into my seat and stared across the room. If people-watching was going to take the place of mindlessly scrolling through Facebook over the next six months, I might as well get used to it.

A large Hispanic man wearing a white chef's uniform strolled by with a cart full of aluminum trays. Steam poured from the tops, evaporating behind the man's back as he walked. He stopped two tables from where I sat and began to unload his cart. The smell of fresh peppers and cooked meat wafted across the room, pulling my face in. I closed my eyes and inhaled as deeply as I could through my nose.

I was hungry—*really hungry*.

When I opened my eyes, I was surprised to find the man leaning against the chair across the table. He stared right at me. "So," he said with a deep, raspy voice, "you like what you smell, huh?"

I was completely caught off guard. His English was perfect, except for a few over-enunciated syllables.

"Y-yeah," I stammered.

"Well, hey," he said, "try one out. See what you think." He tossed a steamy clump, wrapped in a soggy, green corn husk.

I raised my hands in just enough time to keep it from nailing me in the face. "What's this?"

"Tamale," he said. "What, you ain't never had a tamale before?"

I shook my head, embarrassed. "Sorry," I mumbled.

The man shrugged. "No problem," he said, resuming his work across the aisle. "So, it ain't my business, but I gotta ask, what's a nice white boy like you doing down here in San Pedro?"

"I'm, uh, I'm a teacher," I said. It was the first time I'd ever outright said the words.

"Oh, right on!" he said. "Where you from?"

"Missouri," I began. "It's in the middle of the United Sta…"

"Yeah, I know Missouri," he cut in. "I'm a Cali boy myself. Moved down here ten years ago with my family. Here…" He reached down to the lower tier of his cart and pulled out a glossy, red apple. "What's a teacher without his apple?" He tossed it across the table to my outstretched hand. "Hey man," he said, eyeing my food, "give that tamale a shot before it gets cold. I gotta know if I did a good job before this party gets here."

I peeled the husk and examined the entre before me. A fat, wet tortilla stared back. I glanced back at the man, who put his hand out and said, "Go ahead. You might like it."

I opened wide and took a bite. The taste of pork, flour, and chilies flooded my mouth, bringing my chewing to a halt. This had to be savored for every ounce of flavor.

The man simply nodded. "Cool," he said, needing no further confirmation.

He finished unloading the cart and started back for the kitchen, but stopped short. "Well, hey, I think it's cool that you're here to help us out. Teach those kids real good, alright?"

I nodded, trying hard to repress a smile. "You got it."

Hissela arrived shortly after with a tray full of food, followed soon by Jorge. After lunch, we piled back into the Jeep and set out once again into the bustling city.

Our journey brought us to a neighborhood enclosed in a thick, orange cement wall. "Jorge's father—my half-brother—lives here," Hissela told me. "He is out of town, but we will sleep here tonight and drive to Oranado in the morning."

She stopped the Jeep just short of the gate, as an armed guard approached the vehicle. He took Hissela's license and asked a few questions, finally allowing us through.

When we arrived at the house, Hissela led me to a vacant bedroom and suggested that I get some sleep. My coughing had only grown worse during those first few hours in Honduras, and although my mind understood why I had been freezing this morning and was now sweating profusely, my body wasn't adjusting well. I went inside, pulled the curtains shut, and fell into a deep sleep.

Chapter 3

Adaptation

Sleep was exactly what my body needed. When I awoke early the next morning, my cough had all but disappeared; I felt completely refreshed. Following a quick breakfast, Hissela and I said our goodbyes to Jorge and hopped into the Jeep, heading southwest to Oranado.

The hustle and bustle of San Pedro Sula slowly dissipated into the distance. Soon the scenes of Honduras that had already become familiar were all but gone. On the horizon before us, sloping mountain peaks rubbed against the sky. The mountaintops were dressed in puffy white cloud clusters, as if to apologize for their lack of snow.

The highway was crammed with traffic. There were a few cars scattered throughout the mass, but the majority of vehicles were Jeeps and pickup trucks, many of which ferried large groups of people in their beds. Speed limit signs speckled the shoulders, but the traffic didn't seem to notice or care. There was only one law, as far as the drivers were concerned: kill or be killed. To my relief, the horde of vehicles began thinning out as we neared the mountains.

Hissela said that on a straight, flat road, the drive from San Pedro Sula to Oranado would take just over an hour. The actual road, however, was anything but straight and flat. Over the following three hours, the road twisted and turned over jagged mountain bluffs, up and down unpaved inclines, dangerously close to un-railed cliffs, and straight past jaw-dropping overlooks. Most of the road was just wide enough to allow for one vehicle at a time, causing serious problems for those traveling in opposite directions. It was littered with enormous potholes every few feet, often forcing us to drive off-road momentarily, lest we incur serious damage.

Every fifteen to twenty miles, a small town occupied a short stretch of land along the road. Hissela was sure to name each town and give a brief description as we passed through.

"Here is La Entrada, where my mother grew up."

"Now we are in La Jigua. My brother lived here for two years."

"And this is Oranado, where we live," Hissela announced as we entered another small cluster of concrete buildings surrounding children playing in the street.

The town looked no different from any of the others we had passed through that morning. Knowing, however, that this would be my home for the next six months gave it a certain splendor. For the first time, I saw houses and churches, market stands and corner convenience stores, old men and nursing mothers, and it all meant something.

For the first time ever, I was in Honduras.

Hissela parked the Jeep on the side of the cobblestone road, right across from a park. Closing the door behind me, I rested my hands on my hips and took it all in. An ornate Catholic church rose above the small park, enclosed within the square of shops and market stands. Pedestrians crowded the busy street, some buying, some selling, some simply enjoying the park with friends and family. Hissela and I walked into a small store at the corner and were promptly greeted by two elderly women. I didn't understand a word of their Spanish, but their body language suggested that we were expected. They were warm and kind, even offering to take my luggage for me. One woman lifted the hinged countertop, and proceeded to lead me down a small, dimly lit hallway.

At the end of the hall was a door. The woman reached into the pocket of her apron, pulling out a key, which she gently inserted into the handle. A blinding light flooded the hallway, followed by a gust of fresh air, as she pulled the door from its frame. The woman looked back and nodded, then stepped out of the way, allowing me to pass by.

A palm branch flapped against the wall above the door just on the other side. It hung loosely to a treetop, leaning just enough to be seen through the door. Once inside, I was greeted by an entire garden of tropical plants, situated in the center of a stone courtyard. The courtyard was surrounded on three sides by a two-story colonial-style house. A balcony ran the length of the house, leaving a covered walkway for the bottom floor. Heavy, wooden doors lined the walls, leading to different rooms.

I followed behind my guide as she led me to the bedroom in the corner of the first floor. In no time, my bags were unpacked. I fell backward onto the twin bed and threw my arms behind my head, taking in a deep breath of fresh mountain air. *Home at last.*

The moment was soon interrupted by a knock at the door. The second woman from the store greeted me with a smile. *"Quieres venir a almorzar?"*

"Um..." I looked down, desperately trying to sort the words in my head. "I'm sorry...what? Uh...*repita?*"

"Almuerzo," she repeated, pointing upward. *"Quieres comer?"*

Comer! A word a recognized! *Eat.*

"Sí!" I answered. I was hungrier than I'd realized.

I followed her past two wooden doors on the left—other bedrooms, I assumed. We made a turn into the third door. Two laundry baskets, full of clothes, sat beside a concrete reservoir, filled with water. Bars of green soap lined a shelf, hanging just above. *This must be where they do their laundry.*

A wooden staircase took up the back half of the room. My guide slowly climbed upward, holding tightly to the rail, as if her strength might give out at any moment. I followed behind, allowing plenty of space in case of an accident. I didn't know what to expect at a third world hospital, but I wasn't interested in finding out.

The stairs brought us to a kitchen. It lacked any glamor, but it had all the modern appliances you'd expect: a refrigerator, stove, oven, sink, and microwave. Hissela sat at a round table in the corner, quietly sipping a steaming mug of coffee.

"Would you like some?" she asked, turning my way and holding up her mug.

"No," I said. "Thanks. I'm not much of a coffee-drinker."

She chuckled to herself. "I think that may change," she said, bringing the mug to her lips.

Hissela had me take a seat. A plate was quickly set in front of me: refried beans, scrambled eggs, fried plantain slices, and a short stack of corn tortillas. *"Buen provecho,"* the lady said, then turned and walked outside.

Over lunch, Hissela told me more about the house. It was well over a century and a half old and was among one of the first built in

Oranado. The corner convenience store from which we had entered was called a *pulperia*, and the town was full of them. The women working behind the counter were Hissela's sisters.

The trio lived with their elderly mother, who, Hissela told me, was very sick. During those six months in Honduras, however, I never once saw Hissela's mother frown, heard her complain, or passed her without being stopped to ask how I was doing — in Spanish of course. "*Gracias a Dios!*" she would say, pointing upward. *Thanks to God.*

Hissela offered one final piece of advice before I left the kitchen that afternoon: "Honduras, as you know, is very dangerous. You are free to leave the house, but please be careful. It is not a good idea to travel too far from here. And you really should not go out after dark."

I nodded. "Thanks," I said, skipping down the stairs.

"Mark," she said, catching me just before my head disappeared below the kitchen floor. "Many careless tourists have come to Honduras, and many have been robbed and kidnapped. Some have even been killed."

She kept my stare for a moment longer. "Please," she said, "be *very* careful."

Those first couple of days were like a vacation; no stress, no responsibilities, no worries. I wandered through the dirt roads, admiring the mountains and taking in all the Spanish I possibly could.

Oranado, I learned, was part of a small cluster of towns in close proximity to one another. Most of them were populated by farmers and saw little outsider activity, with one exception. About ten minutes down the road sat Copán Ruinas. Copán, as it was usually called, stood out among the rural community. Named for its ornate Mayan temple ruins on the outskirts of town, Copán was widely popular, and brought in tourists from all over the globe. Its cobblestone streets were surrounded on both sides by hotels and local restaurants. Women and children sold trinkets and hand-woven souvenirs beneath pitched tents set up just off the road. The beauty of Copán Ruinas was its ability to capture rural Honduran life amidst its thriving tourism.

My home, Oranado, was the happy medium between the hustle

20

and bustle of Copán and the slow, rural life of the surrounding villages. During the day, the town was abuzz with business. Unlike Copán, however, Oranado was hidden from the tourists. Virtually the only people that knew any English were the school children and a small handful of teachers.

On the morning of my third day, I managed to communicate with one of Hissela's sisters that I planned on buying a hammock in the market. Minutes later, she appeared at my bedroom door with a white, woven hammock, and graciously handed it to me. Since my room was in the corner, I tied it outside between two of the support posts. It hung exactly like a photo in an ad, offering a daily front-row seat to the cloudy sky, draped over the rolling horizon, as the cool wind slid off the mountain slopes and gently blew through the walkway.

I spent a lot of hours those first days in that hammock, reading books, streaming movies on my laptop, and sometimes just thinking. There was plenty to think about: What would school be like? Would I enjoy my time in this country? Would I make any friends? Sometimes I thought about God. More often, I thought about Taylor. Every now and again, I would send her a message from my tablet.

Friday, 8:36 p.m.   Hey, beautiful! How's your day been? I miss you.

Saturday, 9:20 a.m.   Do anything fun last night? I miss you.

Saturday, 6:35 p.m.   Did you make it back to Joplin yet? I miss you.

Sunday, 2:45 p.m.   I'd love to tell you about my first few days here if you've got time. I miss you.

Sunday, 9:57 p.m.   Let me know when you're free to talk. I miss you.

Monday, 9:23 a.m.   Just woke up. The weather's great. I hope you're doing well. Message me back later if you can. I miss you.

Tuesday, 1:15 p.m.   Just thinking about you. I love you. And I miss you.

21

She didn't reply once. *Taylor is a free spirit*, I assured myself. *She's probably out having adventures in the hopes of keeping up with mine. Don't worry yourself. There must be a good reason.* But even though I justified her silence, I couldn't shake the feeling that something wasn't right.

The cabin fever wasn't helping either. As the days passed, Oranado began to get smaller and smaller. By the fourth day, I knew Oranado inside and out. I'd walked by *Cafe de Samuel* on the west side of town, back down the road to the soccer field on the east end of town, and down to the river that marked the southern border of Oranado a hundred times in the span of those few days.

By Tuesday, I was emotionally starved. I needed people. Growing up in Kansas City had made me into a city boy through and through, and an extremely extroverted one at that. Even Joplin, with its modest population of 50,000, began to feel suffocatingly small every few weeks. In those moments, I'd jump in my car and drive as far as possible in any direction. My only boundary was the sky.

But cars were a luxury I didn't have in Honduras. In less than one week, my enormous world had shrunk to the size of a small town in the mountains of Central America, that operated between the hours of 6:00 a.m. and 6:00 p.m. Once the sun set, the day was over. Four concrete walls stood guard against the dangers of Oranado. And in those dark hours, the loneliness began to set in.

The walls of protection began to feel more like the walls of a prison. My only window into the outside world was Facebook, and that only served to fan the flame of my growing depression. I never thought that I would miss home this much. Had the whole ordeal been a mistake after all?

Of the 3,000 residents in Oranado, I was one of two white Americans—*gringos*, as they called us. Donna, another American, also taught at Santa Lucia, and had been doing so for six months prior to my arrival. At the time, she was visiting her family in Virginia for Christmas break. When Hissela told me about Donna the first time, I was ecstatic. *Another American! Someone I can connect with! Maybe this is God's way of taking care of me.*

Then we met.

Donna was double my age, and highly introverted. Being the extrovert I am, this only broadened our social gap. While I pined for games, conversation, and adventure, Donna spent the majority of her time confined to her bedroom, reading or working on lesson plans for school. She was kind, and a very experienced teacher, but there was never much common ground between us. Donna simply did her thing and I did mine.

My only remaining hope was placed in school, which would start the next day. If I could just make it one more night, I would be rewarded with hundreds of kids, a job I'd love, and a cure for the overwhelming monotony of Oranado.

That night, I tried to pray. Whether I was driven by boredom, nostalgia, loneliness, or some emotional cocktail of the three, I couldn't say. It just seemed appropriate.

Um...Lord, hey. I'm pretty excited for school tomorrow. Because, well, honestly, this week has sucked. Not that, you know, I'm not grateful for the opportunity—I am. It's just that...well, I guess I thought it would be different.

I paused, staring out at the twinkling stars from the veranda, then sighed.

"Do you even care?" I said aloud.

Silence.

God, if you're there, I need you to let me know.

Nothing.

Give me something. Anything. A shooting star, a gust of wind, a message from Taylor. Just something.

I waited, but God didn't answer.

Why am I still doing this? I thought. *Who am I trying to impress? If he's real, he'll make things better. If he's not...*

But I was too afraid to finish.

It wasn't the first time the thought had crossed my mind. Before, however, I'd always found ways to fill the emptiness and numb the fear. That night, the feeling lingered. I lied in bed, fighting the empty pit in my stomach until I fell asleep.

Chapter 4

Rock Bottom

Wednesday morning arrived with a 6:00 a.m. alarm and the cries of a hundred screaming roosters. I hopped in the bitterly cold shower and threw on a dressy pair of khakis with a plaid button-up shirt. My backpack waited for me at the door, stuffed with spiral notebooks, pens, folders, and a three-ring binder. I hadn't been given textbooks or curriculum; I didn't even know which classes or grades I would be teaching that semester. The ambiguity was unsettling, but the human interaction that was sure to come put a skip in my step.

Besides, how hard could teaching be, really?

Santa Lucia was built into a mountainside facing a separate range across a small ravine, in which the dirt road ran. Each classroom stood as its own independent building, connected to the others by a paved sidewalk running the length of the property. The rooms were similar in design: each had a long, caged window along one wall, allowing fresh air inside to fill the open space. Every room had at least one electric outlet, but the only light came from the sun peeking in through the window. There were no walls to the cafeteria, except the one that separated it from the enclosed kitchen. It was an open, covered patio that overlooked the mountains. Lunchtime never looked so good.

School began the same way every day: one-hundred and twenty students congregated on the paved soccer court, lined up in single files by grade and gender. Each day, a teacher would stand on the concrete bleachers and give a short motivational speech to the students. Birthdays were always celebrated with songs, and every day the entire staff and student body turned to face the flag and sing the Honduran national anthem. Most days, I simply moved my lips, silently repeating "Watermelon watermelon watermelon." The students were then dismissed to their classrooms, one grade at a time. They remained in the same room for the rest of the day, while the teachers moved from room to room with each period.

There were fourteen teachers that semester, less than half of whom spoke English—myself and Donna included. On the first morning of school, we gathered together in the main office (which doubled as the school library) to divide up the available classes. I walked away with grades six, seven, and eight; responsible for three Reading classes and three History classes.

Before that first day, I hadn't realized that Honduran teachers were addressed by their first names. Henceforth, I became "Mr. Mark." It took some getting used to, but after a few days, I came to embrace it. More times than not, the students would simply call me *"Mee-stair"* and leave the name out altogether.

I had the opportunity to meet with each class individually that first afternoon. With absolutely no pre-planned lessons, I decided to recycle an icebreaker from college. In each class, I wrote three questions on the board:

1. What is your favorite food?
2. What is your favorite color?
3. Who is the cutest person in the world?

Each student was to write their answers on a slip of paper and the class would collectively guess who wrote each. I'd hoped that the game would give me an opportunity to see what I would be dealing with over the next few months.

And it did just that.

The students thought it was hilarious, especially the "cutest person in the world" prompt. I've always enjoyed working with kids, and making them laugh felt great. But it didn't take long before the students began to push the limits. Soon, I was holding on by a thread.

"Come on, guys. Bring it in," I'd say, struggling to regain control. The students paid no attention, each speaking louder than the next to be heard over the others doing the same thing. *How do teachers do this?* I thought. There had to be a way to command respect while establishing myself as "the cool teacher". If Robin Williams could do it in *Dead Poet's Society*, it should've been no problem for me.

When a boy in sixth grade decided to throw his neighbor's book to the floor, however, Cool Mr. Mark did something very un-cool.

"HEY!" My voice echoed off of the cold cinder block walls, bringing the class to a dead silence. "If that happens again, we are going to have problems," I said, pointing my finger at the student. I held his glance for a moment to let my threat sink in. "Do you understand?"

He nodded without a word.

What just happened? I thought, bringing my hand back to my side and running it over my waist, ensuring that my shirt was still tucked in. *Did I really just lose my temper on the* first day *of school? Is this going to be a normal thing?*

I cleared my throat and turned my head to another student, forcing a half-smile. "Let's move on to the next one."

That incident would turn out to be a minor hiccup in an otherwise successful first day of school. Still, the feelings stayed with me throughout the day—the frustration of losing control of a class, the awkwardness of my outburst, the shame of my inability to teach. I hate confrontation. I always have. I knew it was part of teaching—how could it *not* be?—but that didn't mean I had to enjoy it.

I learned two things about being a teacher that day. First, teachers never start out "cool." It's a title hard-earned over time, and not by being a pushover. Second, I learned that I didn't know the first thing about teaching. I was drowning in a sea of ignorance and inability, and if I didn't learn to keep my head above the water, it was going to kill me.

By the time the final bell rang, I was exhausted. I dragged my feet down the hill to the house and fell limp onto my bed. This had not been the day I'd so looked forward to over the last week. I closed my eyes and inhaled deeply through my nose, allowing my thoughts to catch up for the first time all day.

One week in. Let's see: no car, no phone, nowhere to go, no one to see, no contact with Taylor, no proof of God, no hope of liking my job, no friends, no friends, no friends.

I opened my eyes, staring at the ceiling above. "No friends," I mumbled aloud.

I thrive on human interaction. Maybe it's a weakness. If so, I'm willing to accept it. I'm the most extroverted person I know; even after one week, the social isolation was taking a toll. Living in an impoverished Central American country wasn't nearly as exciting as riding the subway in Europe or exploring the gargantuan cities of East Asia—not by a long shot. After a long day at school, a week of learning to survive alone, and realizing that this would be my life for six more months, I wanted—I *needed*—encouragement. And I needed it from Taylor.

It was 8:00 on Wednesday evening. The sun had long since disappeared beneath the earth. I sat alone in my bedroom, quietly planning the next day's lesson when a high-pitched *ding!* broke the silence. The wall above the bedside table glowed as my tablet lit up to display a new notification.

Taylor? I wondered. My prospects were low, but I hadn't completely given up hope.

New Message from Taylor Johnson, the screen read in beautiful, bright letters.

A full week had passed since Taylor and I had spoken. I'd held tightly to her final words at the airport: "I love you." But after a week—*and what a week*—I needed those words again. I wanted to tell her everything. I wanted to hear about everything. I wanted to know that she, too, was counting the days until June. This would surely be the best part of a long, grueling week. I quickly slid my finger across the screen, unlocking the tablet, and opened the message. I couldn't wait to read her words.

(Taylor) 7:47 p.m. We need to talk.

Four little toxic words.

Words of no return.

Words that offer to fix a problem, but have no such intentions.

The first words of a breakup.

This was my greatest fear in coming to Honduras; the one horrible possibility that I never thought would happen. I couldn't believe it. I reread those words over and over in disbelief. I knew what was coming. Even so, I took the bait.

(Mark) 7:49 p.m. Talk about what?

A minute passed. Then five. Then ten. I refreshed the app over and over as the grey typing bubble appeared and vanished repeatedly.

Then came her reply.

(Taylor) 8:00 p.m. I can't do this anymore.

I wasted no time in responding.

(Mark) 8:00 p.m. Do what?

Silence.

(Mark) 8:01 p.m. Taylor, you can't do what anymore???

Confusion and panic overtook me.

(Mark) 8:03 p.m. Please don't do this.
(Mark) 8:05 p.m. Tell me how I can fix this.
(Mark) 8:06 p.m. Where is this coming from?
(Mark) 8:09 p.m. Taylor, why?
(Mark) 8:13 p.m. Please.

More silence. Then, in a sudden rapid fire of messages, she answered.

(Taylor) 8:15 p.m. Mark, I don't know how you didn't see this coming.
(Taylor) 8:15 p.m. We've been having problems.
(Taylor) 8:15 p.m. I've spent so much time thinking about what I should do.

(Taylor) 8:16 p.m. I think we need a break.

(Taylor) 8:16 p.m. It will be good for us.

(Taylor) 8:16 p.m. You may not see it now. It will be better this way, though.

(Taylor) 8:17 p.m. And now you can focus on teaching.

(Taylor) 8:17 p.m. One less distraction.

I read her words over and over. This was all so sudden. Never could I have guessed that Taylor was feeling this way. I needed more; I needed to know why.

(Mark) 8:20 p.m. You told me you loved me at the airport.

(Mark) 8:20 p.m. Those were your words.

(Mark) 8:20 p.m. Five days ago.

(Mark) 8:21 p.m. "I love you."

Silence.

(Mark) 8:22 p.m. Taylor?

The screen froze, then grew blurry as my eyes glossed over. This was the end. I watched hopelessly as she typed her final message.

(Taylor) 8:27 p.m. I'm sorry. I have to go.

And then she left.

I had left everything behind to come to Honduras. I had no friends, no social life, I was overwhelmed with my new job, and the girl that I loved had left me cold, with no explanation. How long had she known that our relationship was over? Why did she wait to tell me until now? What had I done wrong? These were questions that would have to wait six months before having any hope of being answered.

I had achieved my lifelong dream, and it had cost me everything. Rock bottom was a cold, dark place to be. I tried to pray, but nothing came out. There were no words. There were only tears.

"Why?" I finally managed through my sobbing. But there was no answer.

God had abandoned me when I needed him most. And if God was capable of that, then maybe there wasn't a God at all. And if there wasn't a God, then I was truly alone in Honduras.

Chapter 5

Silent God

Mornings in Honduras were nothing short of beautiful. The clouds poured over the tropical peaks like dry ice in a bucket of water. Around 11:00 each day, the sun appeared and drove away the overcast. Until then, though, fog ruled the sky. It brought with it an aura of peace. The cosmos seemed a little smaller in the early hours of the day.

That morning, the cosmos seemed empty.

The morning alarm was again echoed by the army of roosters fighting to be heard. Sleep had provided a blissful escape from the harsh reality of the night before. My eyes stung as I forced them open, dried and stale from a night of tears—an instant reminder. By some random glimmer of hope, I wondered if I might have imagined the whole ordeal in a dream, but a quick scroll through last night's messages revealed the brutal truth.

I moved sluggishly that morning. My eyes kept to the dirt road as I hiked up the hill to school. That day, I kept my instructions short, and my answers shorter. I tried to ignore the pain. I numbed my mind with thoughtless tasks: straightening papers, sharpening a pencil with my thumbnail, drawing overlapping circles and coloring them in. Even so, I was exhausted by my first free period of the day.

I walked to the shed on the far side of the property and sat atop a stump, watching the haze caress the peaks across the ravine. I wondered what my friends were doing in Missouri. I could see their faces in my mind's eye, still fresh from the night before; in my desperation, I had called everyone I could think of to video chat. The reactions had all been the same: "What?! I thought everything was going great between you two."

"Me, too," I'd forced through my sobbing.

I hadn't bothered to ask about their lives. I didn't even mention the grueling week I'd been through. Taylor was all that mattered.

"I'll be praying for you," they had all promised.

"Thanks," I managed. But prayer was the last thing on my mind. I had tried to pray. I'd been trying for months. This is where it had brought me. I was holding onto God by a tattered thread, and I was ready to let go.

Of course, I hadn't mentioned that to my friends during our grainy video chats. What good would it do? Bring Taylor back? Make Honduras more like the U.S.? Grant me super-teaching abilities? As far as anyone in Missouri was concerned, I was praying too; putting my trust in God's plan, and relying on him for hope and comfort. After all, that's what good Christians do.

And yet, there I was, facing a harsh ultimatum: accept God for the bully he was or fall headlong into a godless oblivion.

I had played the religion game long enough. It was time to make a decision. If I was going to walk away from my faith, this was the hour. If I was going to honestly pursue a God I wasn't sure existed, it was time to get serious about it.

So pray. Stop trying to pray and just pray.

"God."

It was all I could get out.

If God was real, he obviously had better things to do than listen to my problems. Besides, how could I possibly tell an almighty God how I was feeling—that I was sick and tired of trying to follow his rules and make everybody happy; that I couldn't even be sure he existed, and if he did, I hated the way he ran the world. These are things you don't tell God, because, well, he's *God*.

I considered singing a song. I've heard it said that proclaiming truth can incite belief. I closed my eyes and pulled the first worship song out of my memory, running through the words in my head.

You give and take away,
You give and take away.
My heart will choose to say,
"Blessed be your name."

It seemed appropriate: God *had* taken away. But I didn't *want* to praise God for that. My heart had chosen to say a lot of things, but

34

"Blessed be your name" was not one of them.

I pulled out my tablet and stared at the glowing screen, as a thought crept in from the back of my head. *Reread the conversation from last night. There must be some clue that this is only temporary*, as if somehow having Taylor back would put all my doubts about God to rest.

The temptation was overwhelming. Against my better judgment, I opened my messages and scrolled upward until I came to the grey speech bubble containing those four words:

(Taylor) 7:47 p.m.   We need to talk.

No sooner had I read it than my stomach began to turn. I immediately tapped the edge of the screen, removing the message from sight. A message from Adam had now taken its place.

(Adam) 10:36 p.m.   Bro, I'm praying for you hard. In six months, we're going to Taco Bell. My treat.

Now a new sickness was rising up, as two words bounced off my skull, echoing over and over:
No friends.
No friends.
No friends.
Not only would I spend my time in Honduras trying to get over Taylor, but I would be doing it without the comfort of my community. There would be no board games, no movie nights, no late night IHOP runs to catch up on life. The people that mattered most were in Missouri. What difference did it make now if I was on Mars?

I need someone to know how close I am to walking away from my faith, I thought. *It's not enough that my friends are praying for me. I'm done pretending that everything will be alright.*

And so, with Adam's name staring back at me, I began to peck at the digital keyboard.

(Mark) 9:18 a.m.   Adam, I'm in a bad place. I'm not sure what

I believe anymore. I need to know how you can trust that God is real and that he loves you.

Then I quickly added,

(Mark) 9:18 a.m. And me.

It wasn't eloquent, but it said what it needed to. I sighed and sat the tablet on the plank before me, waiting, *hoping* that his response would come quickly.

A few moments later, the screen lit up with the words, *New Message from Adam Hartlan*. I lifted the tablet and slid my finger across.

(Adam) 9:23 a.m. I'm sorry this is happening, bro. All of it. Unfortunately, I can't prove God to you. He doesn't work like that. He's a person, not a science experiment. You'll have to meet him face to face to really know. Let him know why you're frustrated. Tell him that you're bummed. Be brutally honest about your feelings and thoughts. Nothing will change if you're not candid. He can handle it, I promise. And if you're paying attention, you might hear him answer. Let me know if there's anything I can do to help. Love you, bro.

Somehow I had expected Adam to give me an equation—a formula to determine God's existence once and for all. At least then I would know for certain one way or the other. Instead, this was his answer. There was no proof, no evidence, no belittling my faith for having doubts. Adam simply told me to be honest with God.

It wasn't the first time in my life I'd heard it, but the idea had always scared me. What are my miniscule problems to the infinite God of the universe? What if I said something disrespectful? What if he didn't listen? What if he did? I'd always believed that God—if there was a God—must have been more interested in my worship than my doubts and questions. Now I didn't know what I believed. If there was no God, then honesty had no consequences; if there was a God, then he already knew what I was thinking. I couldn't wear this mask anymore.

I tried again. "God..." But again, nothing more would come. There was too much to say, to feel, to ponder. I couldn't pray, not like this.

Digging through my backpack, I pulled out a notebook, tore a page from it, and began to write. What followed were the most brutally honest words I had ever written:

Why are you so quiet?

I need to know you're here. I'm tired of feeling like I'm living a lie that I'm too invested in to get out. I'm lonely. I'm confused. I'm thousands of miles away from the closest person that loves me. People tell me that you care, but it doesn't seem like it.

WHY WON'T YOU ANSWER ME

If you're there, I need you. I've heard so many stories of desperate people who found you. So why am I different? Why am I the exception? Taylor left me. Everyone I love is on a different continent. I'm terrible at the job I thought I would love. This entire dream is the opposite of everything I've ever hoped for. And the "Heavenly Father" that I've always been told loves me is deafeningly silent.

So now what? What do I do? Spend the next six months pretending like everything is peachy? And what about after that? Do I just go on for the rest of my life living a lie?

I am alone.

A stranger in a strange place.

If you did love me, if you cared **AT ALL**, you would act like it. If I honestly believed that there was an almighty God who loved me, like **ACTUALLY LOVED ME**, I would be living a completely different life.

I'm desperate. If you're there, I need you now.

It was the first time I had ever hand-written a prayer. There was no *send* button to click, no envelope in which to place it, no one to hand it off to. But if God was there, then he knew; he watched me write it. The deed was done. I sat quietly above my composition, waiting for the sky to split and my Savior to burst from the clouds atop a white horse in a fiery display of glory that would put all my doubts to rest. But the clouds remained woven together in a hazy mist over the mountains yonder.

The silence was soon interrupted by the long chime of the bell. Our session was over. I gathered my supplies and headed off to teach seventh grade history.

God was silent.

Or he wasn't there at all.

Chapter 6

The Village

Less than 24 hours had passed since the world came crashing down around me. I'd come to terms with my isolation and loneliness. I'd been dumped. I'd told God that I wasn't sure he cared about me or even existed. I was utterly drained of all emotion. I didn't want to eat. I didn't want to sleep. I didn't want to think.

I lay in my hammock and stared at the ceiling as the seconds gave way to minutes, and then hours. The roof over my head cast its shadow on my corner of the patio as the hot sun hung overhead. The bustling sound of children playing in the market kept me company, occasionally drowned out by a passing truck blaring merengue. It all meant nothing.

By some senseless impulse, I sat up and stared over the railing of the veranda, meeting the gaze of the green mountains yonder. I loved mountains. I always had.

I stood to my feet and leaned forward onto the railing, letting my arms hang over the other side. The grief was matched only by my boredom. *This is my life now.*

"Screw this," I said aloud. "I'm going for a walk."

My feet ached with every step as I trudged the path in my new boots. They were cheap, and now I knew why. I set out on the same dirt road that led to school. Perhaps that was my destination. But when I reached Santa Lucia, I wasn't finished. The road forked just past the school's barbed-wire gate. Far down the left path stood a giant electric tower. It was hard to tell the distance from my vantage point, so I set off to see for myself. After about fifteen minutes of hiking, I arrived at the base. Past that, the road curved to the right and doubled back, reappearing as it gently sloped up the mountainside.

I kept walking.

The path grew steeper as it followed the incline. My breaths became shorter and deeper, but still I stayed the course. At a point, the path dropped off a cliff with a rushing stream below. It continued on the other side, disappearing into the trees. A rickety wooden bridge hung loosely over the stream, connecting the disjointed road. Only Indiana Jones or a fool would dare cross it.

I kept walking.

I hiked past fields of robusta trees and sugarcane stretching for miles; past cows and bulls feasting on hay; past ditches filled with shredded rubber tires and shattered glass bottles. I hiked until the sun hovered just over the horizon and shadows engulfed the path.

I kept walking.

Up ahead I noticed a beaten trail sprout from the right side of the road. It darted straight up the hill and continued beyond the summit. A barbed wire fence ran alongside the steep cliff to the right side—the only confirmation that this narrow patch of dirt was indeed a path.

I stopped.

Where would this path take me? I wanted to see the top. The desire swelled inside me with each passing second. There was no reason. It would be a foolish venture. I hadn't told a soul that I was going on a hike through the mountains of Honduras alone. No one on planet earth knew where I was. My backpack contained only one book and a few pens, but the pack itself made me a target for thieves. I knew every reason I shouldn't.

But I did.

I'll never have this opportunity again, I assured myself. *What choice do I have, really?*

And with that, I stepped onto the path before me and abandoned my only familiar landmark- the main road.

The higher I climbed, the farther I could see. The mountains seemed to go on forever, well beyond the familiar slopes of Oranado. Once I reached what I thought was the peak, the path leveled out for a few yards and then curved upwards to the top of a new hill, where, again, it leveled out and curved upward.

The sun had just kissed the highest peak when a familiar sound called out from the distance. At first, it was hardly distinguishable from the chirping birds and rustling tree branches. But as I drew closer, the sound grew louder, until there was no question: there were children playing nearby.

The realization came as a surprise. I hadn't seen another person since I left Oranado. Then, from the same direction as the voices, I saw pillars of dark smoke rising from the trees.

Curiosity won me over. I paused for a moment, stooping down to remove my boots and dump two piles of dirt onto the ground, then quickly shoved them back on my feet and started for the mysterious pillars.

Not only had the trail leveled out, it now began to gently slope downward, and even started to look like a genuine footpath stamped out by human traffic. The sound of children's laughter and playful screams grew louder as I stepped deeper into the thin forest. It wasn't long before a small clay structure—about the size of a one-car garage—appeared on the right side of the path ahead of me. Across the path was another. About fifty feet beyond that was another. The mystery was solved: I had stumbled into a tiny community of people living in the mountains.

Pressing on down the dirt path between the row of clay huts, I could see candlelight flickering through the windows. Curious eyes peered out at the strange, overweight gringo who had stumbled into this hidden place. There was no electricity and no running water atop the mountain. Most yards were furnished with a large stone oven. Many were in full use, cooking dinner for the evening. Black smoke poured from the tops, creating the tall pillars that stretched into the sky. A handful of children had been playing when I first entered the village, but upon seeing the strange man, they darted for their homes. The only person still outside was a middle-aged man using a machete to cut the tall weeds growing in his yard. He paid no attention. What did he have to fear?

It took no more than three or four minutes to walk the length of the village. Just beyond the last home, the path turned rugged and dropped over the side of a steep, rocky cliff, vanishing into the woods below. Even if the path continued this direction, I wouldn't be able to navigate it alone. A long hike back to town now awaited me. Knowing that it would be downhill was hardly comforting; in a few minutes, darkness would cover the land completely, and I'd be hiking in it alone.

I turned my back to the cliff and retraced my footsteps up the empty trail through the village. About half way through, I heard the soft patter of feet trailing behind me. I stopped in my tracks and tilted my head slightly to the side. At once, three children dashed to the nearest trees and took cover. I laughed softly. The trees barely covered their tiny bodies. I turned around and started up the path again, followed once more by the sound of sneaking footsteps behind. This time I turned around completely. The children scattered, and one by one peeked out from their trees.

"*Hola*," I offered.

Two children remained hidden, but the third slowly revealed her entire face from around the tree. She couldn't have been more than five years old. She took one small step in my direction, ever so cautiously. I squatted down, bringing my knees to my chest. Looking into her eyes, I spoke again. "*Como estás?*"

The girl was now within arm's length of me. She smiled shyly and brought her arms up over her face. "*Bien*," she replied.

My Spanish vocabulary contained less than fifty words, but I was determined to make the most of this encounter. "*Hablas inglés?*" I asked. I'd learned *Do you speak English?* only two weeks prior.

A huge grin overtook her face and she let out a laugh. "*Inglés?! No!*" she giggled.

"Oh," I sighed, disappointed. "Well, *cómo te llamas?*" If I could learn her name, then perhaps I could earn her trust.

"Maria," she answered with a timid smile.

"*Hola, Maria*," I offered. "*Me llamo Mark.*"

"*Qué?*" she cocked her head to one side.

"Mark," I repeated.

"Mm-ahh-kh…" Maria struggled.

I thought for a moment, then tried something different. "*Marcos.*"

"*Ah, Marcos*," she said with ease.

By now, the other two children had mustered the courage to

stand behind Maria. I asked them their names. "Gabriela," one said. "Cristian," said the other. The conversation was hardly impressive. Through my extremely limited vocabulary, I learned their favorite colors, their favorite foods, and that none of them were currently in school.

In only a few short minutes, I had reached the end of my Spanish knowledge. Just as well. The plum haze of the sky threatened a full blackout soon. It was long past time to be off. I wasn't sure how to say that I needed to leave, so I simply stood up, smiled, and said, "Well, *adios*."

Nothing could have prepared me for what I saw when I turned around. As I had been speaking with the children, entire families had stepped out of their homes to watch. Men, women, teenagers, and toddlers surrounded me on all sides. It was as if life in the village had been put on pause. I raised my hand, offering a wave, and received back, almost in unison, waves from every villager. They whispered to one another as they pointed at me with wide eyes. I was at the center of a hundred pairs of eyes on every side.

I slowly made my way toward the village entrance, careful to avoid any sudden movements that might be perceived as a threat. The whispers grew louder with each step, as if the villagers had realized that there was nothing to fear. I had just as little interest in harming this community as they did of harming me.

Just beyond the village was a cliff that overlooked a valley surrounded by mountains. I stood at the edge, taking in the beauty and reflecting on my experience. Who knows how many, if *any*, of the villagers had encountered a gringo before that evening? They were just as taken by the surprise as I was.

I stared at the mountains in the distance, contemplating my experience, until the cry of a man broke the silence. I whipped my head back toward the village to see a man covered in dirt standing atop a rock, waving a machete wildly in the air—the same man chopping his grass in the village.

"*Ay!*" he shouted. "*A dónde vas?*" I hadn't the faintest clue what he was saying. I lifted my hand to wave, but he repeated himself. "*A dónde vas? A dónde vas?*"

How could I explain that I needed to get back to town? He would never comprehend "Thank you for everything! Your people are very kind. I have to get back to Oranado so that I can be at work on time tomorrow." So I simply shouted back, "Oranado!" in hopes that the message would be understood.

"*Ah! Sígueme!*" he shouted. This time it was obvious that he wanted me to come back to the village. He drew me in with his exaggerated hand gestures and didn't let up. Two options presented themselves: try to outrun the man with a machete or follow his instructions. The sun had sunk below the mountains by now and I knew that the longer I waited, the darker and more dangerous my return trip would be. On the other hand, I'd rather not be chopped up and sent back to Missouri in bite-sized pieces. If he wanted my backpack, I was willing to sacrifice it for my safety, but if this was my final hour, there would be no escaping it.

I slowly made my way back to the man as he continued his gesture. "*Sígueme*," he said again.

"Oranado," I repeated, pointing backward to the path.

"*Sí, sí, a Oranado*," he echoed. "*Ven. Sígueme.*"

He began walking briskly ahead of me, holding his machete firmly at his side. He was careful not to let it graze his leg. I followed along the path through the village, as the entire community, still perched outside their homes, watched. We walked all the way to the dropoff at the edge of the village, where the road disappeared. Without hesitation, the man started down the rocky slope as if it were little more than a worn-out staircase. A few steps down, he stopped, looked back, and said, "*Ven*," again gesturing me to follow.

There was no getting out of this now. I'd committed.

Oh God, oh God, oh God, oh God, I thought in frantic desperation. Where was he taking me?

"*Ven!*" he called again.

I took a deep breath, then started down the cliff.

Each step had to be taken in a very particular form to make it to the bottom of the cliff. Surely this man had made the trip countless times and was well acquainted with the trail. His speed never let up as he hopped from rock to rock. I did my best to keep up, but focused mainly on keeping my balance. He beat me to the bottom in a landslide victory.

When at last I landed safely at the bottom, he took off again, pressing his way through some light brush. A moment later, we were back on the path. We must have walked vigorously for twenty minutes, always headed downward. The last light from the sun lit the earth just enough to keep me from tripping over the tree roots and losing the man ahead of me, although by now he was little more than a dark silhouette against a heavy indigo backdrop.

At last, a familiar site emerged over the treetops. Over the hill, I could just make out the rooftop of the front office at Santa Lucia. The man had led me through a backwoods path straight down the mountain to the outskirts of Oranado. It was dark, and he'd now have to make the hike back to his village with no light. There was nothing in it for him but to help a stranger.

I was speechless.

Searching for the right words—for *any* words—I finally said the only thing I could: "*Gracias.*"

"*Claro que sí,*" he replied.

He reached his free hand toward me, as I took it in mine and shook firmly. He then turned around and began his ascent home, clinging tightly to his machete.

I walked back to town, running through the evening's events in my mind. There was no proof of God in any of it. My faith hadn't been restored. But it was enough to cause me to whisper, "Thanks," to whomever might be listening.

Reaching the house, I inched the back door open, careful not to make a sound and alert my hosts. I ran straight across the courtyard and into my bedroom. My adrenaline was pumping hard now. Someone needed to hear this story.

I snatched my tablet and opened the message app, poking the green circle next to Adam's name. The tablet rang for a moment. Then came Adam's face.

"Mark! No way! Hey guys, come say hi to Mark. How's it going, man?"

The whole gang was there. Their faces quickly filled the edges of the screen as they crowded around the camera to say hello.

"Guys, I have to tell you what just happened."

"Tell us!" came Martha's voice from off screen.

"Alright, so a few hours ago, I decided to go on a walk." I told them the story from start to finish, including every miniscule detail. "And then I ran home and called you guys—well, Adam. It was so surreal. Like, I'm not sure what I expected to find at the top of that mountain, but I definitely didn't think I'd find a *whole community*."

No one spoke. Instead, they stared as if they couldn't believe what they'd just heard.

"So, um," I said, breaking the silence. "What were you guys doing before I called?"

"We were praying for you," Jason said from the left.

I smiled to avoid rolling my eyes. "Oh yeah? What about?"

They looked at one another, waiting for someone to answer. Finally, Adam spoke.

"That you would find community."

Chapter 7

Desperate Songs

I wanted to give God a chance. Plucking me from society and severing my ties with Taylor didn't seem like favors, and the question of science verses Scripture still plagued my mind. But if there really was a God trying to get my attention, I decided I should give him a chance to say what he wanted to say. I at least owed him that after the village. Maybe I was just desperate to hold on to my childhood faith, or maybe God really was making room in my life for something.

The first Sunday following my hike, I decided to go to church. Oranado was littered with churches, but most of them blended right in with the homes. If you weren't walking into a Sunday service, you might be barging in on a family breakfast. There were only two churches in town that I knew of for certain: the giant Catholic Church across the park and the Baptist Church just down the hill from home. I chose the latter for the simple sake of familiarity. My only hesitation was that I'd be going alone.

The cement building could have comfortably accommodated a hundred worshippers. Still, of the thirty-some plastic patio chairs lined near the stage, no more than ten were occupied. Before the tiny crowd, a teenage boy strummed chords on his electric guitar while a large man stood behind the podium leading the congregation in song. There were no hymnals, nor was there a projector; these were sung completely from memory. When the last song ended, a shorter man with a thick, black mustache—presumably the preacher—took his place. He welcomed everyone in Spanish and then gestured at me with an outstretched hand. All eyes turned to look at the clueless gringo in the third row.

The room fell horrendously silent as I twiddled my thumbs. Every second was longer than the one before. How long would they stare at me before realizing that I hadn't understood a word? I finally lifted one hand in a half-wave and forced, *"No hablo español,"* through my humiliation. The preacher caught the hint, gave an awkward laugh, and called the congregation's attention back. Heads turned to the pulpit as I slouched in my seat.

The preacher opened his Bible, cleared his throat, and began his sermon. The echo of his voice filled the room, drowning out the sound of rushing water and chirping birds just beyond the window. Spanish. What had I expected? This Sunday morning was a waste. He might as well have been speaking Klingon.

Is this what church is going to be like for the next six months? Had I thought this through, I would have stayed in bed that morning. I could walk out, but not without being seen. What if he hailed me from the pulpit again?

I reached down for my backpack and pulled out a pen. Perhaps I could use this time to do some writing. Unzipping my backpack, I discovered my notebook was missing. *Idiot, I emptied out my backpack on Friday after school.* All that remained were a few pens, a digital SD card, and a brown leather-bound Bible.

A few months prior, I had started highlighting and underlining in my Bible. After all, nothing makes you look like a good Christian more than a worn-out Bible. That November, I had given Taylor my Bible as a going-away present; church girls love Bibles with graffiti. I decided to buy a replacement Bible a few days before the trip—the same Bible that now stared at me from my otherwise empty backpack as I sat helpless in church. This Bible had no markings, no highlights, no crumpled pages. This could be an opportunity to start fresh.

Pressing my thumb against the gold-lined edge of the pages, I flipped the book from front to back. Where would I begin? What was I trying to find? Hope?

Hope.

That was a good start. Something after Jesus' resurrection. *I'm in a church. Maybe something that addresses the Church...*

Paul. He always had plenty to say about the Church.

I closed my eyes and called to mind every sermon, Podcast, and Bible study I could remember. The answer came almost immediately: Ephesians. Last year, I'd spent one night a week reading, discussing, and praying through the book of Ephesians with five other guys. Our final meeting had us on our knees, praying fervently for the Church and for each other. If there was one book to jump-start my faith, Ephesians would definitely be it.

Again, I flipped through the pages, past the Old Testament, past the Gospels, then came to an abrupt stop at 1 Peter. Too far. Keeping an eye on the top, I grazed the onion leaf pages backward until the page reference confirmed that I'd landed in Ephesians.

Then I started to read.

> "Blessed be the God and Father of our Lord Jesus Christ, who has blessed us in Christ with every spiritual blessing in the heavenly places, even as he chose us in him before the foundation of the world, that we should be holy and blameless before him."

Wait...what? Let's try that again. Refocusing my attention, I started again from the top.

> "Blessed be the God and Father of our Lord Jesus Christ, who has blessed us in Christ with every spiritual blessing in the heavenly places, even as he chose us in him before the foundation of the world, that we should be holy and blameless before him."

But again, I was completely lost by the end. Not only was it littered with personal pronouns, but the entire paragraph was one long run-on sentence.

Having graduated from Ozark Christian College, I knew that Paul played a vital role in the founding of the Christian Church. I understood that he was well educated and well read. His use of words, his sentence structures, every stroke of his quill was highly intentional. Yet, even with that knowledge, I sat in my seat that morning hating Paul. For all his credit, he couldn't even bring himself to shorten and simplify his sentences.

Sitting in that small Baptist church, listening to a pastor give an incoherent sermon and hoping that this would be God's way of revealing himself to me, while desperately wishing I could be anywhere else, I became increasingly frustrated at my inability to do something as simple as read the Bible. I closed the book and set it on my lap.

My eyes darted back to the preacher, full-fledged into his sermon, then began to wander the room. There must be *something* to satisfy my boredom and lighten my frustration. My attention landed on a small chalkboard sign resting on the floor behind the preacher. Written in white chalk were the words, *Psalmos 131:2*. Beneath it was a paragraph in Spanish. Had I been anywhere but a church, I might have shrugged and moved on. But the number might have indicated a verse.

Psalmos...Psalms maybe? Psalm 131:2?

Psalms is easy enough to find. Open a Bible to the middle and you're bound to land in one of its one-hundred and fifty chapters. Spreading my Bible open a third time, I flipped the pages until I found chapter 131. It was a relatively short psalm, so I started at the top and read it in its entirety:

O LORD, my heart is not lifted up;
my eyes are not raised too high;
I do not occupy myself with things
too great and too marvelous for me.
But I have calmed and quieted my soul,
like a weaned child with its mother;
like a weaned child is my soul within me.
O Israel, hope in the LORD
from this time forth and forevermore.

Why *that* Psalm on *that* board? I had no idea. But there I sat, reading it over and over. The words resonated deep within me. I had indeed occupied myself with "things too great and marvelous" to understand. I'd tried to keep God in a box, where he'd have to play by my rules and act in ways that made sense to me. I was no longer trusting in God; I was trusting in an idol, one made in the image of me.

The question of Biblical historicity wouldn't go away. On the contrary, I'd continue to wrestle with it for years. But not that day. That day, apologetics would need to take a back seat. In that moment, I didn't care how old the earth was, how humans got here, or whether the Grand Canyon was the product of erosion or a global flood. One looming question eclipsed them all: *Is there a God and does he care about me?* Nothing else mattered.

Keeping my place with my thumb, I closed the Bible and stared at the stage. When was the last time I'd "calmed and quieted my soul," putting my "hope in the Lord?" Why was it so hard to shut up and let God be God?

Where had things gone wrong? This wasn't Taylor's fault. What did she have to do with the condition of my faith? I was lonely without my friends, but it wasn't the first time I had known loneliness. Honduras was different than I had imagined, but in the end, I was living the dream I had hoped for and prayed about for years. I was struggling in the classroom, but only because I hadn't been given the proper training. This faith crisis wasn't the product of my circumstances—although they hadn't made it any easier. It was the final result of months of separation from a God who refused to behave according to the Gospel of Mark Garnett and His Fundamentalist Commentary of Blissful Ignorance.

I opened the Bible again, but this time I flipped backwards, page after page, until I came to the words in bold letters:

The Psalms: Book One.

Then I read the first verse of the first chapter in the book of Psalms.

Blessed is the man
who walks not in the counsel of the wicked,
nor stands in the way of sinners,
nor sits in the seat of scoffers;
but his delight is in the law of the LORD,
and on his law he meditates day and night.

51

I found a pen and underlined the last two lines. Then, in the margins, I wrote,

God, if you're there, help me to know it.
Make me mindful of you every day and
every night.

I wasted no time moving from the first chapter to the second, and then the third. I put my pen to the page and underlined verse 5:

I lay down and slept;
I woke again, for the Lord sustained me.

In the margin, I wrote one word:

Thanks.

When I reached chapter 4, I stopped dead in my tracks. The words were eerily familiar.

Answer me when I call, O God of my righteousness!
You have given me relief when I was in distress.
Be gracious to me and hear my prayer!

These were the words I had been desperately praying for days. Suddenly, I was reading them in a book written thousands of years ago. I underlined the verse and wrote,

I've known you before — your relief, your
redemption, your hope. God, if you're there,
listen to me now. Answer me when I call.
Show me your grace. Make it undeniable.

Chapter 5 began in a similar way:

Give ear to my words, O LORD;
consider my groaning.
Give attention to the sound of my cry.

And the writer's agony bled straight into Psalm 6:

I am weary with my moaning;
every night I flood my bed with tears;
I drench my couch with my weeping.

I underlined the words, and pressed the tip of my pen to the margin of the page, searching for the words to write. But nothing came— only the heartfelt echoes of that desperate verse in the middle of the Bible. I closed the book, keeping the page with my thumb, and rested it in my lap. I stared hard at the cover, studying the blue paisley stripe stitched across the deep brown leather. I had read the Bible before—not *all* of it, but most. This certainly wasn't my first stroll through Psalms. How had I missed this?

A childhood full of Sunday School, Awanas, and VBS had taught me all about the "plan of salvation" and a handful of fun Bible stories, but no one had bothered to tell me that a day would come when my loving Heavenly Father would come off as a sadist. Summer after summer of church camp had demonstrated God's tangible presence through highly-emotional worship services, but the camp speaker had always neglected to mention that once the spiritual high wore off, God would go back into hiding until enough people came together to sing again and the LEDs and fog machines were turned on. Three years at a Christian College had taught me how to exegete Scripture using the latest Bible software and a Greek-to-English dictionary, but not once did an upper-classman say to me, "Mark, some days, I can't believe in God. I *want* to; I just *can't*."

And yet, only six short chapters into the longest book of the Bible, I was being taught a brand new lesson about God—one that David knew better than most: that sometimes, for seemingly no reason at all, God is just silent. And in those moments, it's ok to cry, to cuss, to hit something, to take a good, hard look at your feelings and doubts, and to be honest with yourself—and with him—about them.

I missed this. It's been there all along, and I missed it.

For twenty-five years, I'd been afraid that I would offend God with my questions, doubts, and anger. Now, unsure whether that God even existed, I sat in a church, reading the same words that had taken root in my mind so many times before—words I hadn't dared to utter. Was my faith weak? Perhaps. If so, then I was in good company with David—the king, the shepherd, the "man after God's own heart."

There are a lot of characters in the Bible. Sometimes their names are dropped once and never mentioned again. Other times, the life story of a single person is stretched over the course of an entire book (or multiple books). Maybe I'm teetering on a minor heresy here, but there are some people in the Bible that I just don't like—and I'm talking about the good guys. They make the worst decisions and say the stupidest things. A lot of holy books in the world present the heroes of their faith as flawless saints. The Bible, on the other hand, is full of screw-ups. And by some divine gag, those are the ones we revere the most.

David is one such screw-up. David, divinely-appointed king over God's people, knocked up a married woman and had her husband murdered before the poor man had a chance to find out. He made a habit of raiding nearby camps and killing everyone inside so that no one could tattle on him. He even found out that his son had raped his daughter and did nothing to punish the boy because David couldn't reconcile the guilt of his own sexual deviance. It's not hard to hate David.

I wish he didn't remind me so much of myself.

I've never committed adultery, but I've dehumanized plenty of women through online porn. I've never killed anyone, but I have wished plenty of people dead for the worst reasons. I've never raided a camp, but I have knowingly taken what's not mine. I've never kept silent at the scene of a rape, but I have breezed right past people on the street in desperate need of social justice. Jesus made it pretty clear that the things we do are manifestations of the state of our hearts. Maybe I get so frustrated reading David's story because I see so much of myself in it.

I think he and I would get along, if we were to ever meet. Not only do we screw up on a daily basis, we're both highly emotional men who process our thoughts through writing. When David went through a dry spell in his faith, he went straight to his scroll and wrote, "Where are you, God? Why don't you care about me anymore?" On days when life was good and believing was easy, David wrote, "Praise the Lord! He's never abandoned me before, and he never will!" David went back and forth between prayers of horrific destruction on his enemies and petitioning for their wellbeing. One day he'd sing, "God and I are intimately close," and the next he'd wail, "God has completely forgotten me!"

If there's one thing I can respect about David, though, it's that the man struggled with his faith throughout his entire life. Yet, we cherish his words as holy, inspired Scripture. If we're to believe that God preserved those Psalms so that men and women could read and sing them over the centuries, then there must be *something* to learn from the words of this emotional, sinful, doubting, hoping, screwed-up shepherd-turned-king that spent his life searching the void for God.

It means that if there is an almighty God out there, I'm allowed to tell him that I'm royally pissed off, that I'm not sure he exists, that I'd rather things happen differently, that he feels distant and unloving. And it means that he listens, and he still loves me anyway.

I opened the Bible back to Psalm chapter six and read the final few lines.

The LORD has heard the sound of my weeping.
The LORD has heard my plea;
the LORD accepts my prayer.

David believed that it was ok to ask hard questions. He also believed that God heard his questions. And he believed that *somehow*, God was ok with it—even in his silence.

Maybe I could learn to believe too.

PART TWO

relearning

Chapter 8
Español

Gzzzzheste díagzzzzzhhhhcon musica degzzzhhh...

The DJ's voice spilled through the tiny speaker, barely audible over the radio static. Time to get up—not that I even needed an alarm anymore. Oranado was home to more roosters than people. They woke with the first light of dawn every morning and notified the entire town. Even if, by some miracle, I was able to sleep through their shrieking, Lora would be sure to let me know I'd missed it.

Lora was a parrot who lived in the tropical garden that grew in the courtyard just outside my bedroom. I didn't see her often—she generally stayed tucked away in the trees and flowers. Not a day passed, however, that I didn't *hear* her. Lora knew one word, and every morning, she screamed it repeatedly with all her might:

"MOMMY! MOMMY! MOMMY!"

No one was sure how it started. Hissela said that she'd always been that way. At first, it was like waking up to the soundtrack of a horror movie. As the days turned into weeks, I eased into it. *It's just a second alarm clock,* I assured myself. *A guarantee that I won't oversleep and miss school. Convenient, right?*

Until that point in my life, I had deliberately avoided waking up before 8:00. In Honduras, if I wasn't out of bed by 6:00 on weekdays, I was running late. Not only was I useless for the rest of the day if I missed a shower in the morning, but it became crucial to spend the first thirty minutes of my day on the toilet. Honduran food wasn't awful, but my body wasn't used to beans and tortillas prepared by unwashed hands. I tried my best to keep from drinking the water... but I couldn't account for what went on behind the closed doors of the school cafeteria.

Even if I wanted to know, I couldn't have asked. Neither of the cafeteria workers (who doubled as custodians) knew a word of English. If I was unsure about the food, or wanted to make a special request, I was out of luck. "Hold the ketchup, please," was answered with a blank stare and a plate of food loaded with ketchup. I was completely at their mercy.

One of my greatest challenges at Santa Lucia was communication, especially with those on staff who only spoke Spanish. I quickly made the acquaintance of the few English-speaking teachers, relying on them nearly every day to translate with my other colleagues. José was one such person. His English was nearly perfect, but for a heavy accent. He understood my sarcasm and threw it right back at me. Best of all, he did everything he could to help me succeed as a teacher. José helped me create my own curriculum, and even set me up with a few private tutoring sessions with students that needed the extra help after school.

I told José just about everything. He knew about my breakup, my ongoing crisis of faith, and my struggle in the classroom. Every day he would sit with me and ask about my life.

"Hey man, how are you doing? Is there anything you need? Do you have questions I can answer—about Honduras? Teaching? Anything, man?"

It was easy to be honest with José. Having spent a few years in the United States himself, he understood the struggles of culture shock. I told him when things were going well and when they weren't. José's advice was always the same: "Do not worry, man. God is going to take care of everything."

The man had a genuine faith even in the bleakest of circumstances. He was shorter than me, with a stocky build. His hair was curly and, more often than not, gelled into place. He was the sort of guy who made jokes and stuck to them like glue until everyone in the room was left to wonder whether he was joking at all. The thing I admired most about José, though, was his genuine concern for those close to him. It was never out of the way for José to lend a hand, an ear, or an encouraging word to his friends and family.

He was happy, *content*. But never so much as when the final bell rang. The best part of José's day was going home to be with his wife and little girl. I envied him. Home, for me, meant being alone for the rest of the evening. I found ways to keep myself occupied, but none of them came with the joy that pulled José out of bed every morning. My nights were filled with movies, books, and the occasional blog update.

A couple of weeks into the semester, I published a blogpost in which I mentioned that Reading was the hardest class to teach; books were scarce in that part of the country, and without them, the task was nearly impossible. I wrote that, in an ideal scenario, I'd like about twenty copies of the same books to use in each class. Almost immediately, someone from my parents' church in Kansas City contacted me. She had read my blog and wanted to help. A church fundraiser was held soon thereafter and the money was used to purchase and mail twenty copies of *Holes*, *Charlotte's Web*, and *The Hunger Games*. It took a few weeks for the books to arrive in Oranado, but when they did, Reading class got a lot easier.

Maybe José was right; maybe God *would* take care of everything.

Shortly following the arrival of my books, I met a girl named Sofía. Only a few months younger than me, she also taught at Santa Lucia, but had been out of town for the holidays when I arrived in Honduras. Sofía Flores García was drop dead gorgeous. She could have been in movies and they would have been better off for it. Her caramel skin was smooth and matched perfectly with her light brown hair, falling just above her shoulders and blowing freely in the wind. Her eyes were deep and dark, and with each smile, they squinted ever so slightly, as if to smile along.

Sofía had never left Central America, but attended English-only schools her entire life. As a result, she had no problem keeping up with my natural speed. I spent a lot of time talking with her when I wasn't teaching. She was funny, and surprisingly easy to talk with. Making her laugh became one of my favorite pastimes. When I was with Sofía, Taylor faded from my mind like a distant memory from another life.

She was the only person that caused me to toss around the idea of living in Honduras indefinitely. What would it look like? How would I survive a lifetime in a country that I couldn't adapt to in a month? Of course I never considered it in any serious matter, but I abandoned the prospect entirely when I found out that Sofía had a daughter and was engaged to be married.

"What's your fiancé like?" I asked her one morning as we sat in the cafeteria grading papers.

"Oh, I do not see him very often," she answered with her soft voice.

"So, when's the wedding?" I prodded, glancing her direction out of the corner of my eye.

She scribbled a letter atop the page with her red pen, giving no attention to my question.

I locked my eyes on her face, leaning forward. "Um, hello? Ground Control to Honduras?"

Now a smile crept over her face. "Yes, Mr. Mark? Can I help you?"

"Sure," I said. "You can start by telling me when you're getting married."

She set her pen down and sighed. "I cannot tell you that, because I do not know."

"Oh, you guys haven't set a date yet?"

"Well, we are not really engaged. We have just been together for a long time."

I tilted my head. "Then why does everyone call him your fiancé?"

Sofía shrugged. "One day he introduced me to his family and he called me his *prometida*—his fiancée—and everybody just accepted it."

"So, does that count?"

She shrugged again. "I am not sure."

"But you do *want* to marry him someday?"

At that, she closed her notebook and gathered her things. "See you later, Mr. Mark," she said, struggling to suppress her grin, then walked away.

No sooner had she disappeared around the corner than José had taken her place at the table. "So..." he said, staring at me with an enormous smirk.

"So?" I raised one eyebrow.

"So, you like Sofía, man?"

I let out a breath of laughter. "She's got a daughter," I said, shaking my head.

"Yes, I know she does," he answered. "That was not my question,"

62

"I'm not going to have this conversation," I answered. "She's engaged. I'm not about to mess with that."

"Ok, man, I understand." He gave me a wink, patted my shoulder, and walked away.

Having weekends off meant finding a way to spend them. I would make constant laps around Oranado (often bumping into my students), occasionally meandering into a restaurant or shop just off the road. Each day, I pushed the limits slightly further, one day exploring the cemetery, the next day crossing the river and hiking along the other side. On my way home, I always cut through the bus station. Men would hold up their hands and yell, "*A Copán, amigo?*" I'd shake my head and continue down the road. *Some day*, I thought, *I'm getting on that bus and I'm going to Copán.*

That day fell on a Saturday, halfway through February. "*A Copán, amigo?*" the man called.

"*Sí*," I said, hopping through the door and plopping down near the back. A few minutes later, we were on our way. And just like that, my tiny Honduran world got a little bit bigger.

After that day, my weekends changed drastically. Every Saturday and Sunday morning, I woke up early, loaded my backpack, and hopped on a bus to Copán. There, I'd spend the day eating at restaurants, wandering through shops, exploring the town, and eavesdropping on the occasional Spanish conversation happening over my shoulder—not that I understood a word. Sometimes just listening felt like progress.

Occasionally, I'd come across an unsuspecting American couple. I'd slither in, coming just close enough to eavesdrop. *Ah, English.* Having José and Sofía to speak with in English was great, but it never compared to the late night video chats with friends back home. There was something refreshing about speaking and listening without restraining my speed and slang—like drinking cold water after a week of nothing but lukewarm soda.

Even on a normal day, Copán was never in short supply of things to keep me occupied. One weekend, the fair came to town. The entire population came out in droves to ride rides, play games, and eat their weight in fried food (with a side of corn tortillas). On another weekend, the fire department celebrated the purchase of its very first fire truck by driving it straight through the plaza and letting the children climb all over it. My favorite, though, was the day that a group of men set up three giant wooden *marimbas* in the park and took song requests from passersby.

But if there was one thing that elevated Copán above the rest of the world, it was the coffee. Until then, I hated coffee. It was bitter and pungent, and it left a horrible taste. Those first few cups in Honduras took every ounce of willpower I had to keep from gagging in front of my hosts. Try as I might to avoid it, though, coffee was part of the very DNA of Central American culture. I found myself drinking it on a near-daily basis, until at last, I began to crave it. I'd drink two cups a day. Then three. Before long, I was walking to the local coffee shop, spending my own money, and slurping down two or three coffees every single day. It was the perfect opportunity to crack open my Bible and do some journaling.

The Bible had become a staple in my day, even if I didn't necessarily understand everything I read. I underlined words and phrases that stood out and wrote questions and prayers in the margins. The yellow spiral notebook that I kept as a backup for school had become my prayer journal. Praying still wasn't easy, but I found that if I wrote my prayers, I was able to engage with God in a way I never could before.

Relearning who God was came slowly. Not only did I discover new things about him every day, I also had to learn how to let go of long-held ideas about him that simply weren't Biblical. So many weeds had to be ripped from my theology.

It wasn't that my faith had been restored, or that God seemed any more or less real than he had when I first arrived in Honduras. Rather, my *attitude* toward God had changed. I'd spent months avoiding the tension that came with the reality of an Almighty God. Now, I faced it head on. If there really was a God listening, then he knew absolutely everything, because that's exactly what I told him; I stopped trying to hide my feelings and questions and instead opened up completely.

Some days were easier than others. There was no formula to determine when believing in God would be easier or more difficult than the previous day. Life just kept happening. When God felt close and loving, I leaned into that feeling and thanked him for it. When the monotony and emptiness of life became overwhelming, I embraced the void, and told God that if he was there, he'd have to fill in the gaps of my disbelief.

The sky never split open. No scales fell from my eyes. I never experienced anything that could be considered "supernatural". And still, something kept me coming back. With every Psalm, I craved God's companionship all the more. So many pleas for help, so many shouts of joy, so much raw pain and exhilarating relief, honest confusion and blissful hope. The air-tight Christianity I once knew was dead; something new was growing from these scattered ashes—something *alive*, something *real*.

Then again, maybe it was just the coffee.

Near the end of February, Hissela's nephew, Jorge, came to visit Oranado. We caught up with each other over dinner one night. I told him about my struggles and successes. He told me that he could never be a teacher. His visit was short, but welcomed. Before he left, he handed me a Spanish Bible and told me to keep it. It was a wonderful gift and I thanked him sincerely for it.

A few days later, I took my souvenir to school to show José.

"Awesome, man," he said, flipping through the pages.

"Now I just have to learn Spanish," I joked.

"How is your Spanish coming?" he asked with a genuine interest.

"Psh, not great."

"No? Why not?"

"I don't know," I sighed. "I thought it would be so easy after living here this long. It's not like I'm not trying. Everyone told me that I would pick it up so fast when I got here. I don't know what I'm doing wrong."

"Hmm," José said. "Well, do not worry, man. God is going to

take care of everything. Maybe I can help you learn. Do you want lessons?"

It was the last place I expected the conversation to go. I was being offered free Spanish lessons from a native speaker. Of course I wanted them! José was happy to help. We decided to meet every Tuesday and Thursday immediately following school. José gave the entire lesson in Spanish. He was sure to speak slowly and use big hand gestures when necessary, rarely using English, if at all. Some days I walked away feeling accomplished; others, I felt hopelessly overwhelmed.

Growing up in the Midwest, I never had a reason to learn a second language. I assumed that all languages were basically the same, with the exception, of course, for the different words used to identify different things. It had never occurred to me that with a different language comes a completely new set of rules regarding sentence structure, conjugation, verb endings, and intonation.

I wish I could say that I came back to Missouri fluent in Spanish. That would be a gross overstatement, though. When I returned home in June, I knew a good deal more Spanish than I had in January. Still, I was nowhere close to the level of competency I'd hoped for.

José's Spanish lessons fundamentally changed the way I saw my students, though. No longer were they just kids; they were brilliant kids. The fact that they could comfortably grasp my words in a foreign language and respond intelligibly blew my mind. I couldn't do anything close to that, and I was double their age. I was still the teacher, meaning I had to take my position of authority seriously. But something changed. Now that I realized how smart they were, I held them with deep respect.

"You're really smart, you know," I told Sofía one day between classes.

"Why do you say that?" she asked.

"Because you speak English so well."

"Well, so do you."

I paused, then shrugged and said, "Touché."

Learning Spanish taught me so much about language at large.

Spanish is so different from English, but they both use a Latin alphabet. It would certainly seem easier to learn one from the other than learning a language like Arabic, which employs a completely different set of characters. Even that seems simple when considering a language like Thai, which not only uses different characters to create words, but depends heavily on the tone of the speaker's voice when speaking. There are even some African languages made up entirely of whistles! Language alone is enough to exemplify the diversity of our world and God's role in it.

It called to mind a private message I'd received in January, the day before I got on my plane. In it, my friend told me that she would be praying for me, and that if I trusted God, I would succeed. "God's love knows no language barriers," she wrote.

I went back to that over and over. If God is all-powerful and all-knowing, then it serves to reason that he knows the inner workings of every language of every person that has ever lived. God speaks English, Spanish, Arabic, Thai, and African whistles, and he speaks them fluently, without so much as a hint of an accent. He hears when his children call— *all* of them. As much as the old fundamentalist preacher would like us to believe that the King James Version is the only acceptable Bible, that's simply not the case. Mankind has been crying out to the heavens for hundreds of thousands of years, and God has met them right where they are.

Learning a second language taught me this in a way I couldn't have begun to understand otherwise. Jesus—at least, the Jesus I met in the pages of my Bible—didn't set any prerequisites for coming to himself. On the contrary, he calls to us in our own language and we follow his voice to redemption.

That's good news. That's the Gospel. It's the love of God. And it knows no language barriers.

Chapter 9

The Airport

"It's so great to see you!" Mom said over the final boarding call announcement. Beside her stood Dad, holding my big, purple bag. We stood amidst a bustling airport. Frantic travelers hustled by on both sides, pushing strollers and dragging suitcases on their hind wheels. An assortment of friends and even a handful of coworkers had gathered around me. But their faces quickly faded into the backdrop when Taylor stepped forward with her arms outstretched.

"I missed you, Mark," she said, holding firm to my body. "I'm glad you're here."

I held her soft head against my beating heart and inhaled the aroma of her clean hair.

Everything was right.

I closed my eyes tightly, squeezing her frame close. But when I opened them again, she was gone; everyone was. There was no airport—only the dark cement walls of my Central American bedroom. I sat up and swung my feet over the bedside to meet a stone-cold foundation.

A deep sadness swept over me, the kind a person can only experience in the lonely hours of the night. I missed my friends. I missed my life back home. And as much as I didn't want to admit it, I missed Taylor.

I went back to the airport countless times over the next few days. Any time life got overwhelming, I closed my eyes and held Taylor in my arms, surrounded by friends and family. It was paradise, matched only by the torture that followed when I opened my eyes and was teleported back to Honduras.

Daydreaming became my new drug. The tiny slice of perfection I'd found consumed me. I tried to fill my thoughts with other things, but every time I thought I was past it, Taylor's memory would charge to the forefront of my mind and hold it captive.

"Alright, class, get out your *Hunger Games* books and let's get started."

Taylor loved the Hunger Games.

"I'm just going to listen to some music while I lie in my hammock."

Taylor and I used to listen to this song together.

"Lunch was great today. I love tacos!"

We had tacos on our first date.

And so, when I could no longer keep it in, I decided to write Taylor a letter. I knew it would accomplish nothing, and probably just make things worse. I couldn't help it, though. Maybe I just wanted to remind her that I was alive—that I was waiting.

I sat down with pen and paper and began by writing her name.

Taylor, it's me.

I asked her how she was doing, recounted a few adventures (and misadventures), told her I missed her, and ended with a sincere wish for the best. At the bottom, I signed my name in cursive. Then, taking hold of my tablet, I snapped a picture and sent it in an email.

The deed was done.

I wonder if she's seen it yet.

It was all I could think about. When would she write back? *Would* she write back? It was the first time in two months that either of us had reached out. Maybe all she had needed was space. What if this letter was the first step in repairing our broken relationship?

My questions would be answered in less than twenty-four hours. Taylor's reply was short and to the point: It was time to move on. She had no interest in keeping in touch. Any hope I might have had for a second chance was ill conceived. We were done. Period.

In an instant, every buried emotion burst to the surface. I became hopelessly aware that I was 2300 miles away from home, and once again, I felt trapped in Honduras. I snatched her thumb drive from the bedside table and shoved it into my computer. Over the next hour, I watched every video, reviewed every picture, and read every note. Then, wiping the drive clean, I ejected it and hurled it across the room.

I never met her in the airport again.

"MOMMY! MOMMY!"

Lora's screams shot through the window screen like a bullet, jerking me from my sleep. I rolled over and closed my eyes, hoping to fall back into unconsciousness, but Lora would have none of it that morning.

"MOMMY! MOMMY! MOMMY!"

"ALRIGHT!" I shouted, rolling onto my back and staring at the ceiling.

Warm sunlight poured through the window, casting shadows against the bathroom wall. Stretching my arms over the sides of the bed, I gave a loud sigh. Why get up? It was Sunday. I had nowhere to be.

My tablet balanced precariously over the corner of the nightstand, where I had carelessly tossed it the night before. Pulling it to my face, I pressed the home button to get a look at the time.

9:03 a.m.

I'd all but given up on church in Oranado. Occasionally I visited the Pentecostal Church down the road to see Santiago—one of my seventh graders—drum in the worship band. But the congregation only met on Sunday nights. I missed my church in Joplin. Oh, what I wouldn't give to be there that morning, among hundreds of people singing in English. Encouragement was what I longed for; hope was what I needed.

I opened the message app and scrolled through. Rachel would be at church that morning. She would surely have her phone with her. It was worth a shot.

(Mark) 9:04 a.m.   Hey Rachel, if you're at church this morning, will you FaceTime me in so that I can watch the service?

I hit the send button and rested my head on the pillow.

Ding!, the tablet replied, almost immediately.

71

(Rachel) 9:04 a.m. Of course!

Rachel called just before 11:00. "Can you hear me?" she said as a blur of colors began to take form. Soon, her face filled the screen. "I'm gonna prop you up on the floor so you can see down the aisle, cool?"

She walked briskly to her seat, swinging me at her side. The music had already started, and the sound of hundreds of voices poured through the tiny speakers. I was soon situated and left to watch as Josh led the congregation in worship. I was home. I closed my eyes and sang along with the crowd, losing all awareness of my surroundings. After a few songs, Randy took the stage and began to preach. To this day, I couldn't tell you what he preached about, but I do remember his final words:

"Take good care of each other."

Randy passed the stage back to Josh, who lightly strummed a few chords on his guitar. "We're going to take some time now to pray with one another," he said. "Why don't you get with those around you and find out how you can pray for them. Then let's take a few minutes and actually do it." He continued strumming as silhouettes in the crowd turned to face one another. That's when the screen began to shake. Had I been knocked over? The ceiling stared at me, then went dark as shadows filled the screen.

"Hey, Mark," came the voice of Adam through the tiny speaker. "I've got some of the guys here with me. We're going to pray with you for a little bit."

I sat in silence, tears streaming down my cheeks, as Matt began.

"Father, we know Mark's not in Honduras in vain. He's worked so hard to be there, but it's been such a hard couple of months. Give him peace—the sort of peace that only you can give a person. Cover his anxiety and his loneliness with your comfort. Remind us to encourage him during this time. But most of all, help him to persevere. Anything he does in your name and your love is no waste of time. We trust you, Father."

One by one, I listened to the voices of my closest friends as they prayed comfort, peace, and perseverance over me. This continued until the voices were overpowered by Josh's singing.

"Thank you," I whispered through tears.

When the service came to an end, Rachel walked around the auditorium to look for friends. "Hey you!" she would call to someone. "Come say hi to Mark in Honduras." No one got away without being pulled in for a quick hello. When she could find no one else, she flipped the screen back toward her own face. "Welp, I guess that's everyone."

"You rock, Rachel," I told her.

"No, *you* rock!" she shot back.

"No, seriously," I told her, "you have no idea how much I needed this today. Thank you."

"Any time, dude," she replied. "Have a great day, alright?"

The screen froze, then went black.

I sat my tablet down and looked up for the first time in two hours.

Chapter 10

Mountain Hike

"You have been here for nearly two months, man," José said, taking a seat in the cafeteria with me. "How are you doing?"

"It's been hard," I said. "Not necessarily *bad*—just, you know, hard."

"What do you miss most about the U.S.?" he asked.

I thought for a moment. "Almost everything."

"Yeah?" he said.

"It's just so *different* here. I'm not saying my country is, like, better than yours or anything. But all the differences make it extra hard for someone like me who's used to something completely different."

José paused for a few seconds and then nodded his head. "I understand, man," he said. "Well, what do you *like* about Honduras?"

I pursed my lips and glanced around. The answer stared me straight in the face. "I like the mountains," I said. "I'd like to go hiking agai..." It occurred to me that bringing up my little adventure two months ago might not be the wisest decision. If my colleagues found out that I had gone hiking through the mountains alone, I may never be allowed out of the house again. Fortunately, José hadn't seemed to pick up on my abrupt stop and didn't press the matter further. I scanned the cafeteria to make sure no one else had caught it. The only other English-speaker in earshot was Enrique. Up to this point he'd seemed disinterested in our conversation. Now he looked up.

"Do you like to hike, Mark?" he asked.

"I love to hike," I said, hoping that the question wouldn't lead to an interrogation.

"We should all go on a hike through the mountains some time," Enrique offered.

"That sounds like a great idea," I said. "Let's go this weekend!"

Enrique raised his eyebrows and looked over to José.

"I cannot go this weekend," José answered. "I have some—how

do you say, *obligations?*—to take care of. But please," he added, "do not let me stop you. There will be other weekends."

I looked back to Enrique. "This weekend?" I asked.

"Yes," Enrique replied. "This weekend."

It came as no surprise that Enrique loved to hike. His long legs and big build were perfect for it. He stood a head and a half over me, towering above José. Enrique was one of the most physically active men I met in Honduras. He filled his weekends with soccer matches, and walked every chance he got. His physical prowess was matched only by his intellect. Not only had Enrique mastered the English language, he was also teaching himself French, and was constantly looking for new books in all three languages. His enormity and intelligence served him well as a teacher. I never met a student that didn't show respect to Mr. Enrique. Even so, the man was thoughtful, gentle, and caring.

Enrique lived in Copán. It was decided that I would stay at his house overnight and we'd get an early start the next morning.

At 3:00 a.m. on Saturday, the bulb above my head burst into brilliant light and Enrique's voice broke the stillness of the night. "Good morning! Let's get going before the sun comes up." I wanted nothing more than to roll back over, to close my eyes and tell him to go away. I couldn't believe that he was ready to go at this hour. "Come on!" he persisted. "Let's climb some mountains!" I let out a creaky moan and dragged myself out of bed with all the strength I could muster. Not even Lora would wake me up at this ungodly hour.

A small breakfast and a quick shower later, the hike began. We followed the cobblestone road out of the city and up through a neighborhood built into the side of the mountain. The road slowly dissolved into a dusty, uneven path that weaved through the trees alongside a creek. We walked for miles by the light of the full moon, until at last, the deep blue sky began to change hues, giving color to the trees and soil. Enrique stopped and examined our surroundings.

"This is a good place to hike," he said, nodding to the right side of the path.

There was no trail, nor anything resembling one. Nothing but trees, rocks, and dirt paved the mountainside. But Enrique's mind was made up, and there was little I could do to change it. He used a stump to hop the barbed wire fence and, without stopping to wait for me, began his ascent up the incline. We hiked for hours, long after the sun came out from hiding. As we climbed the mountain, so the sun climbed the sky, frying our exposed necks like bacon in a skillet.

The trees began to thin out as the terrain grew rockier. Our walking soon became climbing. Neither of us had any way of telling time but for the sun overhead. The mountain seemed to go on forever, as if it was holding up the sky itself. Enrique's pace steadily quickened until, on a particularly steep cliff, he vanished from sight. Finding a foothold and heaving my body upward, I could vaguely make out his form about a hundred yards up. His arms were outstretched and his head held high as he shouted, "We made it!" Forcing myself up the final patch of rock and weeds, I met Enrique at the top of our mountain and fell backwards onto a flat boulder. Our clothes were drenched in sweat. In the thrill of the adventure, neither of us had remembered to pack a water bottle.

For a few precious minutes, we sat in silence, taking it all in. Mountains pushed up through the Earth in every direction, covered in lush, green forests like a fuzzy blanket. The sky was cloudless and almost seemed bluer than normal. I turned to look back, retracing our steps with my eyes. This hike was absurd. I could just barely make out the road, which, from this height, looked like a piece of tattered gold yarn over a green throw rug.

"This country really is beautiful," I said between heaving breaths.

"Yes," he agreed, leaning backwards against his elbows. "It is."

There's an incomparable peace you can only find at the top of a mountain. A soft breeze swept over the forest, rustling the bushes and scattering a flock of birds from the treetops. Their song echoed in the space beneath. No wonder the prophets were always climbing mountains to meet with God. It's hard *not* to feel the transcendence of some otherworldly benevolence from such a vantage point.

In those few minutes, little else mattered. I almost wanted to stay on that mountaintop forever. What a fitting reward for our journey, to grow a beard, build a shelter, and look over God's green earth for the rest of my days. But then, whether by the will of the Lord, the devil, or Enrique's insanity, the dream was shattered.

"We should get going now," he said, hopping to his feet.

"What's the hurry?" I asked. But it was no use. Enrique was already twenty steps ahead of me. I would either sit atop the mountain and make the perilous hike alone, or force myself to my feet and follow behind. *Surely the hike down will be easier than the hike up.*

I was perfectly content to retrace our steps to the dirt road, but Enrique insisted that we go down the opposite side of the mountain. "We are having an adventure!" he reminded me. "Why would we go back the same way?"

True to form, the mountain's spine yielded no paths. However, in place of jagged rocks and rugged cliffs, we were now met with tall, thick grass that grew high above our heads. It clung to our sweaty bodies, making us itch all over. We could see neither the road below, nor the peak above. There was only grass.

After an hour of forcing ourselves through the thicket with no indication that we were making any headway, Enrique let out a sigh and fell backwards. The grass caught his body and held him firm as he wiped the sweat from his forehead. I fell to my knees and closed my eyes. *This isn't fun. This is torture.* He didn't say so, but Enrique's eyes agreed.

Before either of us could say a word, a faint noise caught our attention: the sloshing of running water. It was just enough to revive our spirits. Using what strength we had left, we blindly forced a path through the dense grass, using only our ears as guides. All at once, the grass came to an abrupt end, opening to a wide field overlooking a cliff. And smack dab in the middle, we saw our prize. Water rushed from a PVC pipe poking horizontally out of the earth and collected into a small pool below, trickling from there down the mountainside. There was no explanation for it; we didn't need one.

We raced to the pool and dunked our heads in. Enrique cupped his palms under the falling water and drank deeply. I knew all the reasons I shouldn't do the same. None of them mattered in that moment. As soon as the water touched my lips, I felt born again. We drank and drank, until we couldn't drink any more, and then we took another drink.

I would certainly regret this in a few days. I didn't care. All that mattered was the sweet relief of cold water on my tongue.

It was just enough to get us down the mountain, through the

woods, and back into town. We arrived at Enrique's house late that afternoon, our feet buried in blisters and shirts stuck to our torsos with sweat. The backs of our necks were burnt to a crisp. We smelled like corpses.

I walked into Enrique's guest bedroom to collect my belongings but sat down on the bed instead. Seconds later, I fell onto my back and was dead to the world. It would be another four hours before I woke up, refreshed, confused, and inconceivably sore.

I toddled onto the paved soccer court Monday morning, groaning with each step. José caught my eye and waved me over.

"So man, how was the hike?" he asked, holding his hand out to greet me.

"Horrible," I said.

"Horrible?"

"Horrible," I repeated. "In the best possible way."

He laughed awkwardly. "What does that mean?"

I shook my head. "It was more than I bargained for, that's all."

José shrugged. "So how are you doing, man? How is Honduras? Still hard?"

I reached for my leg, scratching a mosquito bite leftover from the weekend. "In the best possible way," I said.

Chapter 11

Disease

A full week passed without so much as a cramp to suggest that the mountain water had any effect on my body. If anything, my health had improved over the last few weeks. The food that had caused so much physical anguish during the first month had become frequent and common enough that my body had built an immunity to the bacteria thriving inside. Mornings were much easier. I was using far less toilet paper. I even noticed that I was losing weight.

Then, exactly two months after I arrived in Honduras, my body began showing signs of another breakdown. It started with an upset stomach. I thought maybe it was something I had eaten that day. I swallowed a few pills from my stash of medicine. But later that night, my head began to ache. I decided to turn in early for the evening.

When morning arrived, I woke up to a splitting headache and a terrible pain in my gut. I felt pitifully weak and considered staying in bed, but decided to endure the agony in order to make a trip to the bathroom. I made it just in time to vomit multiple times into the shower. With every heave, my head throbbed. There would be no teaching today—not like this.

I told Hissela that I was unable to teach and crawled back into bed. It was a relief to be off my feet, but I found it particularly difficult to get comfortable. My eyelids were heavy, but even blinking proved painful. After an hour of rotating to get comfortable, I finally managed to fall asleep, only to wake up a few hours later feeling worse than before. I spent that entire day in bed, refusing to take a drink or eat a snack. Nothing was going to stay in my stomach anyway, and it didn't seem worth it to test that theory by putting myself through the misery of swallowing anything.

Every time I awoke from sleep, I felt weaker than before. There came a point in the day when I couldn't tell whether I was sleeping or awake. It hurt no matter what. With each turn, I groaned in agony. *This will go away tomorrow*, I kept thinking. But it didn't. The next day was just as terrible, as was the day that followed. I quickly developed an itchy rash that covered my arms and belly. The sickness refused to let up.

Hissela's mother called the local doctor and asked if she would come take a look at me. The doctor was very sympathetic to my condition and treated me gently. In the end, she recommended that I go to the nearest hospital in Santa Rosa to have some tests done. I couldn't believe that this was happening. Going to the hospital was the last thing I wanted to do. It meant two hours in the back seat of a car driving up and down windy roads, followed by God-knows-what once we arrived. I closed my eyes and rested my head against the pillow with a sigh. What choice did I have?

The drive to Santa Rosa was everything I dreaded it would be. Hissela drove as carefully as she could. Meanwhile, I buried my head beneath a blanket and tried desperately to lose myself to unconsciousness. It did nothing to help the anguish. As the Jeep rounded a sharp curve, I barely had time to shove my head out of the window before dry heaving multiple times.

We arrived in Santa Rosa late that evening. The hospital was abuzz with vendors and solicitors along the street. Walking inside, Hissela located the receptionist and had a few words. A moment later, I was led into a large room divided by curtains. I've always hated needles, and when I saw the nurse enter our small enclosure with a syringe, I sighed deeply. This was going to be unpleasant.

Afterwards, we were escorted to a waiting room, occupied by about twenty other people. At one point a nurse walked through, pushing a man in a full body cast atop a stretcher. She parked the man in the center of the room and walked through the swinging doors, making notes on her clipboard as she went. Five minutes passed. Then ten. Staff and patients passed the man without giving him so much as a glance. Had he been forgotten? When his nurse finally returned, she looked completely unfazed. She wasn't sorry that she'd left him unattended in a waiting room; this was typical procedure.

Up to that point, I'd given the hospital the benefit of the doubt. Now, a panic crept into my subconscious, holding hostage any rational thought my mind offered. What awaited me behind those double doors? I'd seen the *Saw* movies—all seven of them. I imagined being forced into a pit full of rusty nails with my hands tied behind my back. "The antidote is at the bottom," the nurse would say. "You've got thirty seconds. Good luck." But of course it would all be in Spanish, so I wouldn't have a clue.

As if being ripped from one reality to another, the dream faded away as Hissela rested her hand on my shoulder. "She says that it is our turn. Are you ready?"

I nodded, taking the nurse's outstretched hand to pull my aching body from the seat. We followed her through the double doors and into another large room filled with dividing curtains.

"*Aquí*," the nurse said, pointing to an exam bed. I took a seat and hunched over, holding my stomach. Four days had passed since I had last eaten anything, and in that time, I had only taken a few tiny sips of water.

She carefully maneuvered an IV into my arm and adjusted a few knobs above my head. I watched as the plastic tube filled with the clear liquid contents of the bag, flowing straight into my arm. *Please God, don't let it be water from the sink.*

A large man pulled the curtain open and took a seat on a rolling stool. He feathered through some notes as he rolled close to the exam bed, his gut pushing out from beneath his white lab coat. "Hello," he said, shaking my hand. "I hear you are sick."

His English caught me off guard. I paused for a moment, letting it sink in, then responded with, "Um...yeah, that's right."

"I'm going to take a look and see what's going on," he told me, pulling a latex glove over his broad hand. The doctor raised my shirt and spread a clear gel along my stomach. It was the first time I'd realized just how much weight I had lost. He pulled a plastic handle with a round tip from the table and began moving it around my torso. As he worked, he watched the monitor into which the handle was plugged. He said something in Spanish and then turned to me with one eyebrow raised. I stared back, expressionless.

"How come you do not know Spanish?" he asked.

"I've only been here two months," I told him.

"This is not a good excuse," he replied. "You need to find a pretty girl and then you will learn fast." I smiled at the joke as Sofía's gorgeous face smiled back in my mind's eye.

The doctor spoke with Hissela in Spanish for a few minutes. "*Ay!*" she exclaimed, bringing her hand to her cheek. The doctor then turned to me.

"There is no doubt in my mind," he said.

I raised my eyebrows, awaiting his diagnosis.

"*Dengue,*" he said, removing his glove.

I'd never heard the word before in my life. "What's that?" I asked.

"A tropical disease," he explained, "carried by mosquitos. It makes your joints hurt and your body break out in rashes. It can also cause severe stomach pain and headaches."

So there it was. The mysterious PVC mountain water wasn't to blame. I had simply crossed paths with one bad mosquito.

"How serious is it?" I asked the doctor.

"Very serious," he said. "Many people die from dengue." My eyes widened. He continued. "But I do not think you should worry. You do not have it as bad as some people do."

"What do I need to do to get better?" I asked.

"Nothing," he said. "Now that you have it, it cannot be treated. You have to let it run its course. How long have you been sick?"

"I dunno," I answered. "Four or five days."

"Hmm," he said. "Give it a few more days and you should be back to normal."

"A few more *days*?!"

"Sorry," he said. "I wish I could help."

Great. I thought. *I have* days *more of this to look forward to*.

Then, a glimmer of hope crossed my mind.

"But now that I've had it, I can't get it again, right?" I asked.

"No, you can get it over and over," he said, jotting something down on his notepad. "It all just depends on the mosquito that bites you. You have been using insect repellent since you arrived, yes?"

We looked at one another silently for a few moments. Hissela shielded her eyes with her hand and shook her head. There was no getting out of this one.

"Do I need to write a prescription for you?" the doctor asked.

"No," I said, head down. "I'll get some from the store."

Four months stood between that hospital visit and my flight home, and in that time, I was one unfortunate mosquito bite away from death—or at the very least, the living death I'd endured over the last few days. Either way, I wasn't interested. I'd be purchasing bug spray as soon as I could walk.

That night we stayed with Hissela's niece in Santa Rosa. The next morning, we were back on the road. When we returned to Oranado, I dragged my feet through the *pulperia* and hurled my body onto my bed.

Enrique and José stopped by the house after school to drop off some hand-drawn letters from the students.

Get well soon!

We miss you!

My body may have been empty, but my heart was full.

I woke up on Monday morning feeling better than I knew was possible. The aches and pains were gone. For the first time in a week, I wanted food. My headache had vanished. My back wasn't itchy. *I'm going to school today if it kills me*, I swore to myself.

It felt like an eternity since I had last seen my students. It felt so refreshing to be standing in front of my sixth grade class that morning. One student, Mateo, stared at me through eyes opened so wide I thought they might pop out. "Mee-stair!" he exclaimed. "You are so...so..." he snapped his fingers as he frantically searched for the word and finally said, "You are no longer fat!" I laughed. He was right. In one week, I had dropped more than fifteen pounds.

"I saw your letters," I told the class. "Thank you for saying that you missed me. I know you didn't mean it, but it still made me feel good."

"No, mee-stair," said Evi. "We did not lie. We like you."

I prepared another sarcastic joke in my head, but as I looked at my students, each nodding their heads in agreement, I cut myself short. These kids knew what dengue was and they had spent the week worrying for their teacher.

There were days I hated teaching. That day was not one of them. Being back with my students brought an unparalleled joy that not even a weekend in Copán could have matched. When school dismissed, I bolted to the stairs and held up my hand to give every student a high five. Then, walking down the hill to Oranado, I headed straight to the supermarket and purchased the biggest can of bug spray I could find.

Chapter 12

Holy Water

Oranado was everything I expected from a small Central American town in the mountains; funny, then, that I never considered that boredom would be my greatest adversary. Most days, I'd rather have lived in Copán. Shops and restaurants stayed open later, the town was far bigger, and there was almost always a concert to see or a fair to enjoy. Unless I had planned otherwise, Copán was where I spent every Saturday, Sunday, and even a few weekday afternoons.

On a particular Sunday, halfway through March, I hopped a bus to Copán, had some lunch, and went for a walk. Before long, I found myself on the edge of town. Not wanting to wander too far from the safety of civilization, I followed the road running along the perimeter. It sloped steadily upward as it drew closer to the range of mountains in the distance.

I'm such a sucker for mountains. Twenty-four years in Missouri had left me with an unquenchable wanderlust for scenery—mountains, beaches, canyons, *anything*. Apart from the occasional sunset, the Great Plains won't show site-seers much to gawk at. Give me tropical mountains over endless cornfields any day.

For as difficult as life was in Honduras, the view was never disappointing. Perhaps that's why I took so many long walks. I found that I could only stare at the mountains for so long before they lured me in. Day and night their whispers called to me, "*Come closer, Mark. Come and see.*" And more often than not, I obeyed.

That afternoon was no exception. As the road continued along the outskirts of Copán, so the mountains grew larger and more magnificent. They softly called my name with each step, promising nothing short of magnificence over the horizon.

At last, the earth around me surrendered; mountains punctured the ground in every direction. I could have explored forever, had I not been on a time constraint. The last bus for Oranado rolled out at 5:00, whether I was on it or not. Still, the day was young. There would be plenty of time to hike.

I pressed on, passing a two-story concrete house built at the base of a rocky bluff. A lawn chair had been propped up in the front yard, holding a man in a faded purple shirt. Hoping to pass him without stumbling into trouble, I picked up my pace, keeping both eyes on the road. That's when I heard him whistle.

I kept on.

He whistled again.

I couldn't keep pretending to ignore it. I could clearly hear him and he knew it. His whistle pierced the air like a gunshot. Taking a deep breath, I stopped in my tracks and turned to face him.

"*Hola,*" I offered, nodding in his general direction.

"*Hola, amigo!*" he called back, leaving his chair and making his way toward me. "*Cómo estás?*"

He shook my hand and proceeded to strike up a conversation. I leaned inward, struggling to keep up, as if being put through a field test of my Spanish competency. He asked who I was and where I was going. I told him that I was an American living in Oranado and that I was simply taking a Sunday stroll through town. He insisted that I follow him up to the house.

I had never seen this man before in my life. What if he was trying to get me alone so he could steal my backpack? Then again, I was already far enough from town that he could have easily assaulted me by now. He didn't seem dangerous, but how could I know for sure? Either way, I had only a split second to make a decision.

I made one rule for myself in this country: if someone invites me, I say yes, no matter what. Time to follow through. I sighed, then, pulling the straps on my backpack, I left the road and followed the man to his house.

Stepping onto the front porch, the man pulled up another chair and motioned for me to sit. He disappeared into the house and emerged a moment later with a plastic cup full of water. It wasn't cold, but drinkable water seldom was in those parts.

"*Cómo te llamas?*" he asked, pulling a chair up for himself and taking a seat.

"Mark," I replied. He tried repeating my name, but had trouble with the 'r' sound. "Marcos," I quickly offered. This was becoming a trend. He gave an, "Ah," and nodded his head. I returned the question in Spanish.

"Marlon," he said.

A woman peering around the door caught my eye. Marlon, realizing what had stolen my attention, stood up and gently took her hand, leading her out to the porch. He introduced the woman as his wife, Sarbia. She reached down to shake my hand and then spoke softly to Marlon in Spanish. He leaned in to kiss her on the cheek just before she disappeared back into the house. Marlon asked if I was hungry. I had already eaten lunch, but it seemed rude to reject his kindness.

Marlon led me inside through the door, which opened into a tiny kitchen. He offered me a chair at the table and the couple began to fill the tabletop with food. Before me sat a large bowl of hot, steaming soup. Surrounding the bowl were tortillas, beans, chopped fruit, and rice. Marlon and Sarbia sat down at the table and placed a few plantain slices and tortillas on a plate for themselves. They took one another's hand and bowed their heads toward the table. Marlon then began praying over the food in Spanish. I couldn't make out every word, but I'm certain I heard my name once or twice.

"*Amen*," he said. "*Amen*," Sarbia repeated. They began folding the tortillas and taking small bites. Marlon started in with a new line of questions. Was I a Christian? I told him I was. He asked if I went to church somewhere in Copán. I said that I had been attending a church that one of my students drummed for in Oranado. He asked how long I would be in Honduras. I told him that I would only be there until June.

About half way through the meal, I heard the sound of children laughing and calling to one another in Spanish. My eyes drifted to the door and were met by three young teenagers. They stopped short of entering the kitchen, surprised to see a stranger at the table. Marlon rose from his chair and stood behind them, placing his hands on their shoulders. These were his children, he told me as he introduced them one by one: Chipi, Elena, and Alejandro. The children stood quietly as we awkwardly smiled at each other, until the oldest reached across the front of his sister and yanked the soccer ball from her hands. She let out a scream as he took off. She quickly chased after him, smiling and calling out threats. The younger brother was soon out the door too. Marlon just laughed. He took the empty dishes from the table and invited me back outside.

As we sat on the porch watching the children play, Sarbia brought us two mugs full of steaming coffee. She handed me one and asked if I would like some sugar. "*Por favor*," I replied. She returned with a spoon full of raw, brown crystals and poured it into my coffee, handing me the spoon to stir with.

Marlon explained that he was a preacher of a very small church only a few miles from the house. He was glad that I was a Christian and that I had such influence in my students' lives as a teacher. He said a lot of other things that I couldn't quite understand with my limited knowledge of Spanish.

Time meant nothing that day. I was completely lost in the experience of it all. It wasn't until my gaze turned to the road and I caught the taillights of a passing bus that I remembered I was on a schedule. The last bus to Oranado would be leaving soon, and I couldn't afford to miss it. I did my best to explain the situation to Marlon. He seemed to understand. He stood up from his chair and I followed suit. His hand rose from his side as he offered one last shake. I brought my hand to his and grasped tightly.

"*Gracias por todo*," I said sincerely. *Thank you for everything*.

"*De nada, de nada*," he replied. I turned around to see Sarbia standing in the doorway, smiling warmly. As I walked through the grassy yard to the road, I heard Marlon shout, "*Adiós, amigo!*" I turned to see them both standing on the porch. The three children paused their soccer game and joined their parents in waving. I smiled and put my hand into the air, then turned around and began my journey back to town.

No sooner had the house vanished behind the cliff than the afternoon began replaying in my mind. Everything over the last few hours was exactly what I had hoped for when I had pictured living abroad. I met new people, dove headlong into Honduran culture, and was welcomed and accepted by strangers.

"Wow..." I said, allowing it all to sink in. "Wow. Wow! That was incredible! WOW!"

Most of the conversation had been lost in translation, but in the moment, it hardly seemed to matter. As I thought about Marlon's kindness, I realized that I had been shown a snapshot of God's Kingdom—or of the Church. Maybe the two are synonymous; maybe they *should* be.

Jesus talked about the Kingdom of God a lot. According to what I could gather from reading my Bible, that Kingdom knows no racial boundaries, no language barriers, no timidity, no strangers, no greed, no isolation in the midst of community. Marlon had exemplified those qualities to someone he had never met before and would never see again. The question of my faith hadn't come until halfway through the meal. I was already seated at his table, eating his food, drinking his precious water. This family hadn't taken me into their home in order to serve a Christian brother. They took me in because they understood what it meant to love like Jesus loved. I could have been Muslim, Buddhist, atheist, or agnostic; I might have been a racist or a criminal; I could have taken advantage of Marlon's kindness and harmed his family. Those possibilities were afterthoughts to Marlon. He simply saw a stranger walking alone and decided to show him hospitality in the name of Jesus.

That's a God I could believe in.

Jesus once said, "If you give even a cup of cold water to one of the least of my followers, you will surely be rewarded." That meant nothing to me before that day. Now, it meant everything. I wasn't in desperate need of water, but Marlon had offered me more than water; he had offered me kindness. That's something I *was* in desperate need of— something I think we're *all* in desperate need of.

I never saw Marlon again, but as I walked away from his house that day, I prayed for him. It took no effort. I didn't even pause to consider whether there was a God to hear my prayer. I just started praying. I told God how grateful I was for Marlon's kindness, and how he would never understand the impact he had on me by simply inviting me into his life for a few short hours.

If God truly is knowable, then I have no doubt Marlon knew him intimately.

I don't claim to know anything about Heaven, if such a place even exists. But if it does, I hope that someday I'll meet Marlon there; we'll sit down at God's giant table and we'll eat and laugh together. I'll tell him how wonderful that day was and how much it meant to me — maybe in English or maybe in Spanish; maybe something completely different. But I don't think we'll have any problem understanding each other.

Chapter 13

Faith

Sofía and I sat across from one another in the cafeteria grading papers, as we did every day. We talked about the differences in our countries, the difficulties of learning a second language, teaching methods that worked and didn't work, and just about anything else that might keep the conversation going. I loved talking with Sofía. I looked forward to it every morning on my walk to school. Sometimes, I even spent my walk thinking up a few conversation topics, just to ensure that we *would* talk. Having a shared free period with Sofía was the best part of my teaching schedule.

It didn't hurt that on Tuesdays and Thursdays, I had two free periods back to back. Sofía would join me for the second, but the first was shared with twenty kindergarteners and their teachers in the cafeteria. Since they only spent half the day in school, they were given a light breakfast each morning.

Kindergarten was when the students first began learning English. Most of it was repetition-based. Every day before breakfast, Mrs. Ana would lead the children in a prayer:

"Dear Lord," she said, slowly and clearly.

"Deeer Looord," the children repeated in unison, with closed eyes and clasped hands.

"Thank you for this food."

"T'ank you f'r dees fooood."

"Please bless my mother."

"Please blase my marthar."

"And my father."

"And my fahdeer."

"In Jesus' name,"

"Een Jeezooz naaaame,"

"Amen."

"Ameen."

There was hardly anything cuter in the world.

When Sofía arrived, I asked her if she had ever seen the kindergarteners pray for breakfast.

"No, I have not," she answered, pulling a notebook and folder from her bag.

"Sofía," I said, "you have to come out here some time and see it. I swear, it's the best part of my day."

"I am sure," she answered. "Victoria likes to pray in English at home."

"Your daughter is so stinkin' cute anyway," I said.

"Yes, I know," Sofía let a sly grin creep across her face. "I take that as a compliment."

"Well, you should," I said.

I was inspired by the Kindergarteners, especially little Victoria, Sofía's daughter. If they could pray in English, what was keeping me from praying in Spanish? I tried it a few times. Struggling to find the right words and having no accountability to find them, however, I quickly gave up. In the midst of my frustration, I began to question whether or not it was even worth it. Did God think I was using him as an educational punching bag? Would he even care about the things I prayed in a language that I hardly knew?

Certainly, prayer had been a game changer for me, even if it was done almost exclusively through journaling and making notes in the margins of my Bible. But in the moments of frustration and confusion, my shaky faith grew even more unsturdy. Sure, I ran to God after the breakup with Taylor, but where else did I have to run? Besides, I went to a very specific God: the Christian God—namely, Jesus Christ. What if I got it wrong? What if the Bible got it wrong?

My faith tank never quite made it to 100, but it got close a few times. I didn't have rock solid proof of God, but there was no denying that my life had changed ever since I began making time in my day for him. There was a peace in knowing that I wasn't alone in my loneliness; a joy in knowing that someone cared—someone that could do *something* about it, even if that *something* was to suffer alongside me. Time with God was refreshing, like water for my soul.

Still, if I was honest with myself, believing in an invisible God seemed like a bit of a copout. What religion *doesn't* conveniently believe in an unseen God? So instead, I left the Psalms and skipped the rest of the Old Testament entirely. I went straight to Jesus. Here was "God" in flesh and blood, seen by thousands, immortalized in four historic accounts. What did he say and do?

I quickly found a pattern in my Bible: Jesus healed a lot of people in those last three years—anyone who's ever read the Bible could tell you that. What I hadn't realized, though, was the emphasis Jesus put on faith when it came time to heal.

"So-and-so is sick," people would tell Jesus. "Will you come heal them?"

Jesus would often reply, "Sure, just have faith."

Sometimes it happened after the matter. "Your faith has made you well," Jesus would say after he healed a person.

That revelation threw me for a loop. How did Jesus expect these people to have such strong faith, especially after a lifetime of living in the fear that God had abandoned them? Was Jesus, in essence, telling people, "I'll heal you or your buddy, but only if your faith is rock solid with absolutely no doubt at all"? That idea seemed so contrary to the God I thought I knew—the God who longed for a genuine relationship with his children, regardless of their lingering doubts.

So I tried. I tried to have "better" faith; I tried turning a blind eye to anything contrary to cookie-cutter Christianity; I tried to "just believe". But the more I did, the further backwards I fell. I didn't want to relive my crisis in January all over again, but Jesus was clear: I had to have faith. And the more I dwelt on that, the harder it became to have any faith at all.

If faith was something I had to *do*, then I was terrible at it. And if the only way to get better was to have stronger faith...well then, I was hosed.

When I could no longer stomach Jesus' impossible faith standards, I left the Gospels altogether and journeyed farther into my Bible, coming face to face with my old nemesis, Paul. I tried reading Ephesians again, but the memory was too fresh. So I went one book backwards: Galatians.

If the tone of Ephesians was *encouragement*, then the tone of Galatians was undoubtedly *anger*. The whole book was driven by Paul's disdain for what the Galatian Church had become. In a nutshell, they had traded grace for morality; somewhere down the line, they abandoned their interest in God himself and started focusing on the rules and regulations of contemporary mainstream religions.

Paul didn't like that, not one bit. He was so worked up, in fact, that he suggested the men promoting circumcision should go ahead and chop off their own enchiladas.

Paul was a big fan of grace. For him, if there was anything we could do to earn God's favor, then Jesus' life and death were a colossal waste of time and resources. Salvation, in Paul's mind, was something only Jesus could provide, and we can only obtain it by abandoning our own efforts and accepting that fact.

That sounded a lot more like what Jesus was talking about. And in that light, I began to see that maybe doubt isn't the opposite of faith. Maybe when Jesus said, "Your faith has made you well," he wasn't talking about something we *do*, but something we *don't do*. Maybe faith is less synonymous with words like *strength, courage,* and *assurance,* and much closer to words like *surrender, stop,* and *give up.* Maybe instead of calling strong Christian warriors to put their faith to the test, Jesus wanted people to realize just how weak they were; to understand that outside of him, there was nothing they *could* do. Maybe "Just have faith" could be restated, "There is *nothing* you can do to help yourself, but I can do *all* things. If you trust me more than yourself, then you will see my power."

That sounded much more like the Jesus that Paul (and even David) knew, and it sounded an awful lot more like a God who longs to draw his people close to him.

This new revelation didn't solve all my problems or answer all my questions. But it did make faith in Jesus a lot easier. For the first time in my life, I stopped *trying* to have faith, and I *let* Jesus do the heavy lifting for me.

"*Papá,*" I began to pray on a daily basis, "*ayúdame a tener fe.*"

Father, help me to have faith.

PART THREE

reassuring

Chapter 14

Family Dinner

Poverty ravaged Honduras. Even in my first few months, I saw some of the worst living conditions imaginable. The farther from society a town or village was, the less people had. In the mountains, especially, scores of people were accustomed to living without luxuries like running water, electricity, cars, even clocks.

Money was hard to come by in that part of the country. Even those who lived in town and put in an honest day's work still struggled with their finances. Because of this, Santa Lucia was facing a severe financial crisis. The school had only been open a few years, and was desperately treading water. Paychecks were delayed one week, then two weeks, then a month. Even when I was paid, it was often far less than I had earned. I knew the struggle and tried not to grumble. I didn't have a family, house, or bills to worry about like most of the teachers. Still, as my stash of *limperas* started to dwindle, my anxiety began to grow.

Money wasn't my only worry. As March drew closer to April, another matter seized my attention: Honduran Immigration Law. I hadn't bothered to research the legal procedures in Honduras before moving. (Because why would I do something so obviously important?) I'd simply decided not to worry about it until the time came.

I'd heard that most countries will give their visitors a grace period of ninety days—no work visas, no extra fees, no legal trouble. I knew a few teachers and missionaries around the globe, though, who had found loopholes to extend their stay. Most simply left their host country every eighty-nine days and returned after a three-day period, renewing their allotted time. Having made no other plans for my trip, I adopted that option for myself, hoping I wouldn't fall into any trouble. After all, Oranado was only thirty minutes from the Guatemalan border.

I knew that Central America was no stranger to tourism. To the north was Roatán, a tropical Caribbean island, and the port of hundreds of cruise ships annually. To the south was Tegucigalpa, the country's capital and a hot spot for American mission trips. Even Copán Ruinas, without so much as an airport, brought in tourists from around the globe. Surely I wouldn't be the first alien to spend over ninety days in Honduras.

Half way through March, I brought the matter to Hissela's attention. She mentioned that there might be a cheap way to extend my stay by signing some papers at the Immigration Office in San Pedro Sula. I was willing to go along, but I decided right then that even if the government didn't require me to make a trip across the international border to Guatemala, I would find an opportunity to make the trip before June.

A couple weeks before we left for San Pedro Sula, José invited me to his house for dinner. I told him I wouldn't miss it for anything. He drew a rough map of Oranado on a piece of notebook paper, labeling a few major spots, then drew a big circle around his house.

"It is just across from *La Terraza* restaurant," he told me. "You will see it, man. My neighbor has a pig tied to his porch."

Ah, Honduras.

I left my house that evening and followed the dirt road that cut through Oranado, walking all the way to *La Terraza* before I stopped to look across the street. Sure enough, there was the pig, tied to the post of a two-story concrete home. In the house's shadow rested a tiny hut made from dried clay and cement. The door was wide open, allowing chickens to casually walk in and out of the house as if they owned the place. *This must be it.*

I walked up and stood in the doorway, giving my eyes a moment to adjust to the dim interior. José sat in a rocking chair just inside, whittling a small block of wood. He looked up and exclaimed, "Hey, man! Come in!"

I walked through the doorway and stood in a small living room. The walls were decorated with intricate wooden carvings and paintings. "Cool," I said, pointing to one. "Where did you get all these?"

"I made them," he said as he set the block down and stood from his chair.

"Wait, like, you painted them, or...?"

"Painted, carved, imagined. I did it all."

"Wow. These are really good. You know, if you came to the States, you could probably sell these for a lot of money."

"Maybe," José said through a suspicious grin, eyeing his artwork.

I leaned in. "Something you'd like to share with the class, Mee-stair?"

He turned to me and shook his head. "Nah, man."

"Alright, fine," I said. "I know something's going on in your head, though. I can read you like a book."

At that, José cracked. He slapped his knee, losing himself to laughter. "Oh man! I have never heard that before!"

I smiled and shrugged. "It's not that funny..."

"Yes it is! *I can read you like a book!* Hahahahaha!!!"

Two heads peeked out from around the corner, obviously curious to see what all the commotion was about. José composed himself, still wearing an enormous smile. "Here, man. Come meet my family."

José introduced me to his wife, Anahí, who stood over the stove frying bananas, and his beautiful three-year-old daughter, Claudia. Her curly, brown hair bounced on the back of her little white dress as she ran into her daddy's arms and gave a loud squeal of joy. José lifted her up and pointed to me. "*Este es Mr. Mark*," he said into her ear. She covered her face with her tiny hands and timidly peeked out from between her fingers.

"I think she can read you like a book," José said, laughing at his own joke. I rolled my eyes. He bent down to set her onto the floor, and in no time she was off again, galloping and singing without a care in the world.

José gave me a complete tour of his home: a bedroom with just enough room for a twin bed, which he shared with Anahí, and a small mat in the corner for little Claudia; a closet, containing a single toilet and nothing more, separated from the rest of the house by a thin curtain; and a tiny kitchen packed with dishes in every available inch, leaving just enough room for a stove. Behind his house sat two concrete reservoirs full of water for washing clothes and doing dishes. Two plastic bowls

103

leaned against the side.

"Are those dog bowls or something?" I asked.

"What, these?" he asked, picking one up. "Nah, man. I mean, maybe they could be used for that. I do not have a dog, though. I use these to shower."

"To *shower*?"

"Yes." He demonstrating filling a bowl and dumping it over his head. "It is the only shower I have."

I watched him in disbelief. "What do you do when it's cold out?"

"I hurry," he answered with a smile.

"*Listos?*" a voice called from inside.

"*Si, amor,*" José called back. "Are you ready, man? Let's go eat."

We crowded around the small table in the corner as Anahí brought out each dish: scrambled eggs, fried bananas, refried beans, and of course, corn tortillas. José reached down and pulled Claudia up to the chair.

"*Muchas gracias,*" he said, as Anahí took a seat.

We loaded our plates using our bare hands. "Here man, take some of this," José said again and again, dropping off handfuls of food onto my plate.

"Yeah, yeah, thanks. I'm good," I said, finally pulling my plate out of his reach. Claudia pointed and giggled.

"She likes you, man," José said.

I smiled back and took a bite.

"So," José started in, "Did you ever figure out what to do about your time here?"

"Yeah," I said. "I think so. We're going to the Immigration Office in San Pedro Sula in a couple weeks to get things sorted."

José relayed the information to Anahí in Spanish, then turned back to me. "Who is 'we'?"

I swallowed my bite. "Me, Hissela, Enrique."

"Enrique is going?" he asked.

"He's Dominican," I said. "Remember? He has to renew his visa to stay in Honduras. We're just gonna make one trip for both of us."

"Ahh," José said, again turning to Anahí and translating. "*Mark tiene noventa días*...ninety days, yeah?"

"Yep. Then it starts over and I have ninety more."

He continued his translation, then took a swig from his clay mug. "You *want* to stay and teach, then?" he asked, setting his mug on the table.

I paused to consider the question.

"Honestly," I began, "No. I don't. And look, I know that sounds terrible. I just miss my friends and family back home. I love the students, and I'm going to finish strong, but if I had to do it all over again, I really don't know that I would want to."

José set his mug down. "Man," he said, reaching for another tortilla, "You have a good life in the U.S. You can go to college and find jobs and make money for your family. I envy you. Those things are hard to do here."

"*You* have a job," I said.

"Yes, of course" he agreed. "But I cannot pay for the things that are important."

I swallowed the small bite of banana in my mouth. "What kinds of things are important?" I asked.

José looked at his daughter and softly placed a hand on her back. "You know, man," he said, "Claudia was very sick when she was born. We took her to the hospital and she is doing better now, but I am—oh man, how do you say when you owe a lot of money?"

"In debt?" I offered.

"Yes, exactly," he said. "I am very 'in debt'. Sometimes I am afraid that she will get sick again, and then what will I do?"

I set my fork on the table and looked around. This tiny hut was all that José had. He didn't even own a car. He was completely reliant on a job that was anything but reliable, doing everything he could for his family. But still, it was just barely enough.

José wasn't oblivious to the realities of a third world country. He knew what kind of life I had in the U.S. And yet, by some miracle, he was happy—not thrilled, but happy. José knew peace in a way I never had.

I looked him in the eye, searching for the words. "José...I..."

"Do not worry, man," he interrupted. "God is going to take care of everything."

If I had half the faith that this man had, I could command every mountain in Honduras to throw itself into the Caribbean, and there wouldn't be a moment's hesitation.

"*Muchas gracias por la cena*," I said to Anahí. My Spanish was awful, but I knew enough to thank her for dinner.

She smiled back. At last, something she understood. "*De nada.*"

Chapter 15

Immigration

"How long have you lived in Honduras?"

"A few years now," Enrique said, turning his head toward the back seat. "I met my wife here. I am trying to gain citizenship, but they keep pushing it back. Once a year, I have to report to Immigration."

"Sounds like a hassle," I said.

Enrique snickered. "Oh, yes. This country makes nothing easy. I love my wife, though. And my children only have only known Honduras all their lives. So I will keep making the trip."

Hissela nodded in affirmation, keeping both hands on the wheel and eyes on the road. Together, we'd ventured out from Oranado to make the trip to San Pedro Sula. Hissela and Enrique sat in front, talking back and forth, mostly in Spanish. Every now and again, someone would ask a question in English, giving me a chance to join the conversation. It was only a matter of time, though, before they slipped back into Spanish, leaving me to my own thoughts in the back seat.

Just as well. The road through the mountains had some of the most beautiful scenery in Honduras. Watching the mountains fly by kept my interest for most of the drive. Only when we were on level ground with the rugged country behind us did I give any heed to my nausea. I considered taking a nap. It wasn't long, though, before we were in the thick of traffic. We merged onto a highway, and in no time, we had reached San Pedro Sula.

Hissela said that we had made good time and asked if we would like to stop for breakfast. I prepared for the usual meal of beans and tortillas, but was surprised when we pulled into the parking lot of Dunkin Donuts. It was nothing impressive, but to a guy who hadn't seen an indoor, air-conditioned, chain restaurant in three months, it might as well have been *L'Astrance* in Paris.

By the time we got to the Immigration Office, it was swarming with people. The line stretched out the door and around the side of the building. By the looks of it, many of them may have camped outside the building for days.

"What's this about?" I asked, closing the Jeep door behind me.

"Immigration," Hissela answered.

"The line, I mean."

"Yes," she said. "These are people hoping to get passports and visas."

I looked again. There were hundreds. "*All* of them?"

"All of them. And most will be turned away without a good reason."

Enrique said nothing, but wore a melancholy expression as he scanned the line with his eyes. His gaze fell to the pavement as we drew closer to the building. Of the hundreds of people trying to get out of Honduras, Enrique was the only person trying to get in.

My eyes darted from Enrique to the line. Bored and tired faces stared back, watching as the trio passed the line altogether and entered through the double doors. The line continued inside, slithering back and forth, squeezing itself into every open inch of the massive room. It poured into a large waiting area, where every metal chair was occupied. Surely there wouldn't be enough time in a day for these people to speak with the Immigration Office—perhaps not even a week. And if they did, then what?

Hissela stepped up to a desk and spoke with the secretary.

"Why do they get turned away?" I said, lightly bumping Enrique's   arm   with   my   elbow.

"What?" he said, turning to me.

"These people. Hissela said that most of them will get turned away. Why?"

"Ah, yes," he said with a nod. "The government in Honduras does not care about most of its people. They see them as numbers, not as humans. Some may have enough money to offer a bribe. But most are poor and cannot. And so they will not be allowed to leave."

"Honduras is a democracy, though, right? I mean, can't the people work together to change things?"

"Well, yes. But if the president continues to buy votes from poor

108

people in the mountains, he will continue to win."

"And nothing will ever change."

"Exactly."

I scanned the room again. So many people; so many dreams.

"It's not fair," I said.

"No," Enrique said, looking out over the crowd. "It is not."

Hissela turned around and waved us closer. "Follow me," she said.

We followed Hissela in silence as she led us down the hall long hallway past the desk. "This is where you will go," she told Enrique, pointing to an office door. Enrique knocked and entered with permission.

The door closed behind him, as we continued down the hall. Near the back, just before the emergency exit, the hallway turned left and opened wide to reveal an office space. A man in a black uniform sat behind a desk near the turn, filling out paperwork.

"*Hola*," he said, looking up from his desk. "*Cómo puedo ayudarle?*"

Hissela spoke quickly and fluently. I couldn't make out the words, but they were obviously talking about me, periodically glancing in my direction and making gestures.

After a few minutes, Hissela thanked the man and we started back down the hallway.

"Good news?" I asked.

"Oh yes," she said. "This will be easy to take care of—easy and cheap."

"Yeah?" I asked, curiously.

"It is just like you thought. He said that you can leave the country for three days and when you get back, your ninety days will be renewed," she explained.

"So, um, does that mean I'll be going to Guatemala?" I asked, desperately trying to restrain my glee.

"Yes," she said. "I have some friends in Chiquimula. You can stay with them. As soon as we get back to Oranado, I will call them and you can take a bus there."

I'd given up trying hiding my smile. I was going on another adventure in a matter of hours! I rode that wave of joy all the way down

109

the hall, halting just outside Enrique's office door. In a few minutes, the door opened and Enrique emerged holding a stack of papers.

Hissela made sure everything was set and then started toward the double doors to the parking lot. I slowed my pace, allowing Enrique to catch up.

"You get everything taken care of in there?" I asked.

"Hmm? Oh, yes," he said, as if stirred out of a dream. "Everything is taken care of. I will be back next year."

My smile faded as we rounded the corner into the lobby. Hundreds of eyes followed us to the door, then fell back to their hands as they continued to twiddle their thumbs in quiet tedium.

Hissela held the door for Enrique, who, in turn, held it open long enough for me to take the handle. I stopped just short of the cement and turned around, scanning the room one last time. "I'm sorry," I whispered. "I'm sorry." Then, turning around, I let the door close behind me.

We drove back to Oranado the next day.

"Go get your things and meet me out here," Hissela said, parking the Jeep just outside the *pulperia*.

My excitement had drowned out the realities of the day before. I ran to my bedroom and threw a few shirts and some toiletries into my backpack. I made sure to grab my passport from the bedside table drawer before leaving again. Then, locking the door behind me, I bolted through the garden, back through the *pulperia*, and hurtled into the Jeep. Hissela gave me instructions as we drove to Copán:

"My friends will pick you up when you get to Chiquimula. Do not get on a bus until after you have *made sure* it is the right one. Be careful; Chiquimula is much bigger than Copán and it can be very dangerous."

We pulled up to the bus station and, after saying thanks and goodbye, I hopped out of the Jeep and into the bus. I yanked a pair of earbuds from my backpack and connected them to my stowed-away tablet. This trip called for Spanish music.

Take me to Guatemala, Enrique Iglesias, I thought, succumbing to the big, stupid grin that slowly crept across my face.

Chapter 16

Last Resort

The people of western-Honduras used the word *bus* in a few ways. *Bus* sometimes referred to the elongated vehicle with aisle seating, like the average school or charter style. Most often, though, when someone used the word *bus* in that part of the country, they were referring to a twelve-passenger van that ferried up to twenty-five people from one town to the next. There was never room to move on the bus; if someone needed off before the intended stop, everyone had to file out and squeeze back in. Sweaty bodies pressed up against each other like sardines in a can. On most trips, children and small women had to sit on laps. Sometimes people would even stand on the passenger step and hold tightly to the roof as the van sped down the uneven roads, passing other vehicles with only inches to spare. The smell was atrocious and the heat was intolerable, but the fee was only ten lempiras (about fifty cents), so no one complained.

The "bus" to the Guatemalan border was no different, except twenty lempiras more expensive and far less crowded. It must have been more advantageous to go one town over than to hop the international border.

We sped down the paved road, deep into the mountains, passing Marlon's house on the right. For the first time in weeks, I found myself in a place I had never been. Small, shanty homes were built randomly into the mountainside. The closer we came to the border, though, the fewer homes we passed.

Finally, the bus pulled into an empty lot beneath a metal canopy and the driver turned the engine off. I waited for the passengers ahead of me to exit the sardine can on wheels and then made my way to the door. I passed three folded tens to the driver on my way out and stepped out of the way, eyeing the road ahead of me. A single armed guard stood watch between two boom gates about a hundred feet apart. That small patch of no-man's land was all that stood between me and glorious, foreign soil.

"Make sure you go through customs before trying to cross the border," Hissela had instructed me. I looked around. There were only two buildings on the Honduran side. The first was covered in signs for mobile providers, candy, and cigarettes; no doubt it was a *pulperia*. The other building was lined with glass windows and flew a giant Honduran flag above its door. *This must be* it, I thought, pulling the handle on the glass door. A blast of cold air erupted from inside, sending a shiver over my body.

I stood at the entrance of an open lobby. Ropes hung from stand-up poles leading to the row of desks lined along the back wall. The lobby was empty, but for a stocky female guard, three travelers in line, and me. The guard sat behind the desk in the far corner, checking passports and collecting fees. The first person in line was a middle-aged Hispanic man. The two others were gringo hipsters with dreadlocks. I took my place in line and waited patiently as each traveler spoke with the guard in fluent Spanish. All three were admitted without issues.

When I arrived at the desk, the guard asked me, in Spanish, why I was going to Guatemala. I told her that it was a three-day vacation. She nodded and placed her palm upwards. I handed her my passport, which she quickly flipped through once. Then twice. On her third try, she examined each page carefully, then glanced up at me, snapped the passport shut, and slid it back across the desk. This wouldn't work. I offered a confused look. Tomorrow, she said, my ninety days would expire. I tried to explain that leaving the country and returning after three days should solve that problem—at least, according to what the Immigration Office had told me yesterday. No, I was told. I would have to leave this part of Central America altogether. The closest border I could cross for my plan to work was Belize—a journey that would take two days each way by bus. If I went to Guatemala today, I wouldn't be allowed across the border to Honduras when I came back.

I picked up my passport and slid it into my back pocket, my head hung low in defeat. I wouldn't be going to Guatemala today. Without a cell phone to get things sorted out, there was only one place I *could* go: back to Oranado. I pulled a twenty and a ten from my wallet and passed them to the bus driver, taking a seat in the back. He was noticeably confused; hadn't I been on this same bus only a few minutes ago?

We made it back to Copán with just enough time for me to sprint across town and catch the last bus to Oranado for the day. I ran through the *pulperia* and searched the house, finding Hissela in the kitchen.

She was shocked. "What are you doing here?! You are supposed to be in Guatemala!"

"I know," I managed through my panting. "They said if I cross the border today, I can't come back to Honduras until I've left Central America altogether. The closest country I can go to is Belize, and I'd have to stay there for three days."

"What? No! You cannot do that. It is too dangerous for you to go that far alone."

"Well, they won't let me back across the border again if I go tomorrow."

"*Ay, Dios mio,*" she said resting her face in her palms and shaking her head.

"So, um...what do I do now?"

"You go to Guatemala! The Immigration Office said that it will renew your ninety days."

"Ok, I get that," I said. "But what if they made a mistake?"

"You think the Immigration Office made a mistake?"

"I don't know. But even if they didn't, the border police won't let me back into Honduras if *they* think I'm breaking the law, even if they're wrong. All I know is, every day I stay here after tomorrow counts against me. I don't want trouble."

She sighed, then muttered something in Spanish and stood up. "Why is this happening?" she said. Then, without another word, she left the room.

Um...what exactly am I supposed to do now?

The clock on the wall thundered with each tick of its hand. Every second wasted at the table ushered me closer to the deadline. I stood up, walked across the courtyard, and sealed the back door behind me. I could think of only one place to go.

"What's up, man?" José said, spotting me from the front step of his home.

"I'm in deep trouble."

"Really? What happened?"

I told José the entire story. "I don't know what Hissela wants me to do. I don't know what I *need* to do." I sighed. "I'm scared."

"Hmm," he thought aloud. "Well, do not worry, man. God is going to take care of everything."

"Yeah, fine," I said. "You keep saying that, and like, ok. Maybe he will. But that doesn't mean I won't go to jail or be fined some outrageous amount of money I don't have."

He thought about it for a moment, and then said, "Ok, man, I have an idea. I know someone who might be able to help us out."

José pulled out his cell phone and dialed a number. After a quick conversation in Spanish, he told me, "We have to go to Copán. Tonight."

Not twenty minutes later, we hitched a ride to Copán with José's brother, who just happened to be headed that way. By the time we arrived, the sky was dark. It was odd being in Copán after sundown. I'd made sure to be back in Oranado by 5:00 every day. Lamps and rope lights hovered over the town, illuminating the uneven roads. Warm light spilled from open windows, speckling the mountainside like the Milky Way. José moved quickly through the cobblestone streets while I trailed behind.

At last, we reached our destination: ViaVia—a hotspot for tourists, complete with restaurant, hotel, and tourism office. We breezed through the entrance, passing the hostess, and took our seats at a booth in the corner of a dark, unoccupied lounge. Flickering candles lit the shadows, bathing the room in a grim ambiance.

I ordered a Coke from the server as she walked by. José settled for water. We sat in silence for a few minutes, until finally I looked at José and spoke just above a whisper. "Who are we meeting again?"

"We will know when he gets here," José answered.

"Wait, you don't know him?"

José shook his head. "I have never met him. But he has a reputation. He can help with these kinds of problems."

I slumped in my seat. What was I getting into? "What time will he be here?"

"I do not know, man," José answered quietly. "Hopefully soon."

Our drinks were dropped off and, once again, we were alone.

The next person to enter the room was a giant of a man. His fedora brushed the top of the entryway as he stepped into the lounge. The flickering candlelight illuminated the man as he walked closer. Thick, black hair peeked out from the top of his half-buttoned shirt. His shaven face revealed a chiseled jaw, as if his skin had grown over a brick. He scanned the room and then made his way to our corner. Removing his fedora and placing it on the table, he took a seat across from us.

The man looked at José and spoke a few words in Spanish. José nodded and said, "*Sí*." The man turned his glare to me and extended his gargantuan hand across the table. We shook and then the discussion began. I couldn't keep up with the Spanish, and as anxious as I was, I didn't try.

After a few minutes, the conversation drew to a close and the two men shook hands once more. He replaced his pitch-black fedora atop his head, then left the room. I downed the remaining Coke in my glass bottle and turned to José. "What did he say?" I asked.

"Come on," he said. "Let's go outside."

José was silent as we retraced our steps down the road to the park. He stopped and looked me dead in the eye. "Look man," he started. "This guy can help you. But it will not be...how do I say...legal."

"What do you mean?" I prodded.

"Ok, man," José seemed to be stalling. "He said that he will meet us here tomorrow. You must bring your passport and three-thousand lempiras. He will bring your passport back in two or three weeks and everything should be taken care of. We cannot ask questions."

I didn't know what to say. I couldn't even begin to process what I had just been told. I brought my hand to my forehead and closed my eyes. "What do you think I should do, José?" I asked.

José sighed. "It is your choice. I will not respect you less for your decision."

"What choice do I have?" I said, throwing my hands into the air. "If I don't leave Central America tomorrow, I'm screwed!"

My arms fell to my side as I dropped onto the concrete step leading to an empty stage. I stared out over the plaza in silence. Oranado would be quiet and peaceful by now; Copán, meanwhile, was wide awake. The locals passed through the park going about their business. Two or three gringos sat at the opposite end of the stage, laughing and joking with one another. I envied them. They had no worries in the world. I was American; I wasn't supposed to be worried about deportation.

"We have to find a computer," I told José. "There *has* to be another option."

José thought for a moment, then said, "Ok, I think I know somewhere."

We set off down the road, arriving at a tourist lounge. The sign on the wall boasted laundry, coffee, books, souvenirs, and computers. We found the front counter and asked the barista about the computer. After paying a small fee, we were handed the access password on a small slip of paper.

"*Tienen una hora*," the barista told us. *You have one hour*.

And so began the search. I scoured the internet, looking for something—*anything*: legal loopholes, traveling tips, immigration procedures. One dead end led to another. *What am I even looking for?*

A small, grey box in the upper right corner of the screen counted down the remaining minutes. I was almost out of time, and still no closer to any helpful information than I had been nearly an hour ago. It was hopeless. I closed the browser and slumped into my chair. The lounge's homepage now stared back at me. Five or six popular websites were linked near the bottom. Having all but given up, I slid the cursor to the link labeled *Facebook* and clicked.

I mindlessly scrolled through my news feed—a small consolation to distract me for those final few minutes. Everyone seemed to be doing just fine that evening. John had a new job. Kristen and Samuel were in a relationship. Aaron had spent the day at the beach, and had pictures to show for it.

What a fun, carefree day that must have been. Of course, it was nothing out of the ordinary for Aaron. That man loved the coast. In the few years he lived in Missouri, it was all he talked about.

"Why did I move back? I miss the beach."

"Back in Florida, we'd be swimming right now."

"I hate this snow. Give me sun and sand, baby!"

I'd known Aaron since I was a teenager. Back then, he was the youth pastor at my parent's church. Over the years, our relationship had evolved from teacher-student into friends, even with ten years between us. Aaron was always looking for opportunities to get back to Florida, so when a ministry position in Bradenton opened up, he snatched it, making the move with his wife and two children. We'd kept in touch over the phone, even once or twice in the last three months, but I hadn't seen him face to face since the move.

It would be a long shot, but I was out of options. I clicked on Aaron's name, opening a message tab, and started typing.

(Mark) 8:47 p.m. Hey dude, I have a sort of crazy question.

The grey bubble appeared for a moment. Then came his reply.

(Aaron) 8:47 p.m. What's up?

(Mark) 8:47 p.m. Can I come stay with you guys in Florida for a few days?

(Aaron) 8:47 p.m. Sure. When are you thinking? Sometime after you get back from Honduras?

I hesitated, then, holding my breath, I typed one word.

(Mark) 8:48 p.m. Tomorrow.

I hit the enter key, and waited for a reply.

The bubble was back. He was taking longer than before. Had I been too audacious to invite myself to his home on such short notice?

Finally, a message appeared.

(Aaron) 8:50 p.m. Sure!

Takeoff was scheduled for 11:25 the next morning. The plans were set: I would pay José's brother 500 lempiras to drive me to the airport in San Pedro Sula that morning. Aaron would pick me up in Tampa that evening, and I would stay with his family over the next three days. When I returned to Honduras on Thursday, I would take a charter bus back to Oranado.

"How much will the bus ticket cost?" I asked José.

"I do not know," he answered. "I have never used this service before."

"What if I can't afford a ticket?" I returned. "You know the school hardly ever pays us on time. My money is running short."

"I know, man," he agreed.

"Aren't you going to tell me not to worry?" I asked. "That God is going to take care of everything?"

"Man," José said, putting his hand on my shoulder, "he already has."

José caught a friend walking to his truck just outside the park. He asked if we could hitch a ride back to Oranado, and the man was more than happy to help. The truck bed was already filled with passengers. I recognized one of my sixth grade students sitting near the front. "Hey, Evi," I offered.

"Hello, Mee-stair Mark," she replied, then turned to José, sitting to my left. "*Hola, Mee-stair José.*" He gave a smile and a wave. "What are you doing in Copán?" she asked.

We briefly explained the situation as the truck began to pick up speed. As my body bounced in the pickup bed, my eyes wandered upward. The stars were bright that night. I smiled to myself, realizing that the next time I'd see the night sky, I would be on American soil.

"Evi," I said. "Make sure to tell the class where I am this week, ok?"

"Ok, Mee-stair," she agreed.

I looked back at the stars, twinkling in their simple elegance, and added, "And make sure Miss Sofía knows where I am too."

José shot me a look.

"Ok, I will," Evi said. "Have fun in the U.S."

"Oh, I will," I assured her.

José leaned in, placing a hand on my shoulder as he whispered, "I can read you like a book."

Chapter 17
Sabbath

I was up before the sun that morning. My body begged for more sleep; it took every ounce of willpower I had not to give in. I'd spent the night packing and video chatting with my parents to let them know the situation. They assured me that they would be praying for me, and even loaned me the money to buy my ticket. The stress of it all still lingered, but the morning brought with it a glimmer of hope. I had no plans over the next three days, except to rest and act as American as I could.

I wrote a quick note to Hissela, explaining my plans, and walked up the stairs to place it in the kitchen.

I'm excited, God, I prayed, retracing my steps down the veranda to retrieve my backpack. *I guess you already knew that. Which means you probably also know that I'm worried about money for my bus ticket. Um, I guess I'll cross that bridge when I come to it. I'm trying to believe that you'll take care of everything like José keeps saying. It's just hard, you know? Trusting when I can't see you. For now, um, well, thanks. I'm really looking forward to the next few days.*

I pulled the knob to close my heavy bedroom door, but paused when I heard a creaking sound from behind it. I peered around the door to see my American counterpart, Donna, standing outside her bedroom, still dressed in her nightgown.

"I'm sorry, Mark," she began.

"You're...sorry?" *What on earth could she be sorry for?*

"Well, I didn't mean to eavesdrop, but it was late and I was having trouble sleeping. And, well, I heard about your trip."

"Oh, right. Sorry if I kept you up late."

"No, no," she said, waving it off. "It wasn't *you.* I couldn't get to sleep. It happens from time to time. Anyway, I know you're stressed, so I was praying for you and, well, I felt led to give you a little something."

She walked to me and held out a fist. I cocked my head to the side and brought my open palm up to her hand. She dropped a small, folded piece of paper and closed my fingers over it. "I hope this helps. I'll continue to pray for you this week," she said, then turned around and walked back into her bedroom, closing the door behind her.

I opened my hand and looked down to see a triple-folded one hundred dollar bill. José was right. Again.

To this day, I can't understand why some people hate flying; it's just my favorite. I can't stand getting on an airplane and sitting next to the one person who feels terribly inconvenienced by the whole arrangement and can't help but inform everyone around them. Sitting next to someone who refuses to open their window is just as bad. I guess for some people, the modern miracle of flight isn't worth the energy it takes to turn your head slightly and watch as the aircraft defies the laws of gravity, offering stunning views that mankind has only dreamed of for millennia. Even when I'm tired and would rather sleep, that intrigue alone is enough for me to open the window and admire the beauty.

"Would you like an aisle seat or a window seat, sir?"

"Window, please. And, if it's not too much trouble, please seat me away from any fuddy-duddies that might be flying today."

Clouds can be beautiful from the ground, but at eye level, they're breathtaking. Looking out the window, I couldn't help but wonder, *Were we meant to see this? This is a privilege only birds and angels should have*. Incredibly, until the last hundred years, it had been. I wondered if some day people will speed past intergalactic nebulas light-years away and ponder the same things. There's nothing in the beauty of a bird's eye view that proves the existence of God, but there is something poetic that almost transcends the need.

When I fly, everything else in my life becomes infinitely less important. In those few short hours I spent over the Gulf of Mexico, the last three months faded away, and the next three days became blissfully uncertain. All that mattered was the sensation of being thirty thousand feet above the Earth and marveling at the boundless canvas of water and mist below.

The first major difference that caught my eye in Tampa was how green everything was. Bright, perfectly mowed grass stretched out in long, symmetric rows alongside the paved runways. The second surprise was how straight and proportional the buildings and roads were. Everything had a purpose, a reason. In Honduras, people built around the earth; in the United States, the earth was an obstacle to be overcome. Even amid these thoughts, one repeated itself like a broken record in my head: *I'm home*.

I sent Aaron a quick message from my tablet and waited beneath the canopy over the curbside doors. Minutes later, a black car pulled right up to the sidewalk. I watched my reflection disappear as the tinted window receded down into the door and a new face stared back.

"Welcome back to America!"

It was a forty-five minute drive from Tampa to Aaron's home in Bradenton—a perfect opportunity to catch up with one another. Aaron told me about the church he now worked at, and I told him stories from Santa Lucia. Now that we both worked with students, the conversation seemed to carry itself.

"What are your plans while you're here?" he asked, as we drove over the Sunshine Skyway Bridge.

"I don't really have any," I told him. "I didn't even know I was coming to Florida until last night. I really just want to rest."

"Well, we've got a bed ready for you," Aaron said. "Feel free to do all the resting you want."

"Thanks. I don't really mean *sleep*, though. I guess it's more that I don't want to, like, *try*."

"What do you mean?"

"You know, I don't really fit in down in Central America. That's not necessarily a bad thing. I mean, I knew I would stand out in a place where I'm the only person who doesn't speak the language and has white skin. I'm learning the cultural norms and all, but, well, I just need a break—a few days where I can act like an American without worrying about what other people will think."

"This week'll be good for you, then," he said. "I will warn you, though, Bradenton attracts a lot of Europeans this time of year. You might not feel as American as you would in Missouri."

"Bradenton is also three hundred dollars cheaper than a flight to Missouri would've been," I told him. "Trust me, dude, the fact that every sign we've passed has been in English is more than enough. As long as the beaches aren't full of hairy, naked people, I'll be just fine."

"Sorry, man," he said. "I can't make any promises."

Everyone was asleep when we arrived at the apartment. Aaron showed me to my bedroom and made sure I knew that the kitchen was open to anything I wanted.

"Sleep in as late as you want tomorrow," he added. "I've got the day off, so when you get up we can hang out. Maybe we can go kayaking in the river if you're up for it."

"That sounds awesome," I said. "Thanks again for helping me out."

"No problem," he answered. "Thanks for coming to hang out in Florida."

The next day, Aaron called a friend to ask if we could borrow his kayak. The man was happy to help. We drove across town to pick up the kayak and headed north toward Manatee River.

"What do you want for lunch?" he asked.

"I really don't care, man."

"Yes you do," he shot back. "This week is yours. What are we eating?"

"I dunno," I said. "I just want...something American, I guess."

"Come on, give me more than that," he prodded. "You're getting too skinny. My goal is to fatten you up before you go back. You've gotta help me out. It's been three months and you can't think of *anything* you want?"

"Let's just get something really greasy and unhealthy," I said.

"Five Guys it is," he said, nodding to seal the deal.

We pulled into the lot and took our place in the short line of vehicles, inching forward, and finally arriving at the drive-thru speaker.

"What're you getting?" he asked.

I scanned the menu. Months ago, I would have splurged without a second thought. Now, I wasn't even sure how much my body could handle.

"Just get me a cheeseburger and fries," I said, then added, "Small."

"*Small?!*" he looked at me in disgust. "You're too skinny, boy. I've got three days to put some pounds on you, and that's what I plan on doing."

"*HiWelcomeBacktoFiveGuysCanIHelpYou,*" a muffled voice poured through the speaker.

Aaron leaned in. "Yeah, can I get a cheeseburger? Make that a double. And an order of fries to go with that. Large." He looked at me with a smirk.

"*OkDoubleCheeseBurgerLargeFryWhatToDrink.*"

"Water," I said firmly.

He turned to the speaker. "Dr. Pepper. Large—no, extra large. Whatever the biggest size you have is."

"Dude…"

"Shut up. You'll get what you get and you'll like it."

"*OkAnythingElse.*"

"Yeah," he continued. "I'm gonna get…"

I rolled my eyes. It was his money; if he wanted to spend it on hospitality, I couldn't stop him.

We ate our body weight in fried goodness as we made our way to the river. When we arrived at the parking lot on the riverbank, we slung the kayak into the water and carefully stepped in.

"Have you ever done this before?" he asked.

"Nope," I replied.

Aaron gave me a quick tutorial in rowing and steering. Having lived in southwest Missouri, I'd been canoeing plenty of times; kayaking was fairly similar. Unlike a canoe, however, the kayak sat low in the water, threatening to heave us into the river if we leaned too far to one side or the other. We didn't talk much for the first few miles; most of our attention was focused on perfecting our balance. Then, after finally getting the hang of it, Aaron broke the silence.

"So how's your walk with the Lord?" I heard him ask from behind as my paddle entered the water.

What a youth pastor.

"You know, it's kinda funny you ask that," I said, turning my head to the side and raising my voice. "A lot's happened in the last few months, even before coming to Honduras."

I filled him in on the events leading to my crisis: how college had lead me to question the things I'd believed all my life, but had been too afraid to allow myself to ask. I told him about the night that Taylor dumped me over Facebook, forcing me to admit that my life had swung out of control. I mentioned the advice Adam had given me, to simply be honest with God, and how it had been monumental in learning to reconnect with God. I told him that believing never came easily or naturally, but that I was trying to trust that God was bigger than my doubts—that he would fill in the gaps when belief was impossible. I said that reading my Bible had become a staple in my day; that when I actually engaged it with questions and doubts, tears and laughter, notes and prayers, it began to feel more like having a conversation with an author than simply reading a book.

"Not gonna lie," I said. "I still struggle with a lot of it—*most* of it, really. But I think it's a good place to be. At least, right now."

Aaron agreed. "It sounds to me like God might have brought you to Honduras to pull you away from all the distractions. Maybe he was trying to get your attention, and the only way was to force you out of your comfort zone."

"Maybe," I said. "I've definitely thought about that. You know, it's weird. I've always taken my own faith for granted and just assumed that everyone else knew something I didn't."

"Yeah?" he asked. "What do you think now?"

I brought my paddle just above the surface of the water and sat in silence for a moment. "You know that story in the Bible where God tells Elijah to go stand outside because he's about to pass by? First, there's an insane wind and everything starts breaking apart, but God isn't in the wind. And then there's an earthquake, but God isn't in the earthquake. And then there's a fire and God isn't in that either. And then when it all calms down, Elijah hears a still, small voice, and that's actually God."

"Yeah, First Kings," Aaron said.

"Well, I think I've spent my life looking for God in the wind and the fire and the earthquakes, and the reason I've been disappointed so many times is that he's usually not in those things. I can force myself to see what I *think* is God, but if it's not really him I'm seeing, then I'm getting the wrong idea of who he is.

"When I first got to Honduras, my life started crashing down around me. But I can't say I think *God* was behind it all. I mean, maybe. But sometimes bad things just happen, you know? It really wasn't until everything calmed down that I was able to refocus and see God for who he is."

Aaron let my words sink in as the kayak drifted peacefully down the river. Only the buzzing of flies and the occasional chirp of a passing bird broke the stillness of the moment. I shook my head and laughed silently.

"What's up?" Aaron asked.

"It's crazy, man, you know? I grew up believing in a God who was always ready to fight the devil and save the world from evil. But when I actually *read* the Bible, I see a God who lives with his people and bleeds on a cross—a God who suffers *with* his people."

And with that, the conversation was over. The sun hid behind thick, puffy clouds as a soft wind blew cool air from the bay. Everything would have been perfect, but for one thing.

"Dude," I managed, "I hate you for ordering so much food."

My body was cramping in ways I hadn't felt since I first arrived in Honduras. I was ready to explode.

"Alright," he said. "We can turn back. There's a restroom close to where we parked." He inserted his paddle straight into the water, causing the kayak to make a sharp turn in the opposite direction.

"No, man," I said. "You don't understand. I'm going to have to jump into the river for a few minutes. I can't hold it."

"Well, that's up to you," he told me. "But before you make that decision, I should let you know that this river is known for having lots of sharks."

The thought that this river dumped into the Gulf of Mexico, only a few miles away, hadn't occurred to me before that moment. I clenched every muscle in my body and peered over my shoulder with a scowl.

"This is your fault," I said. "You and your extra large double cheeseburger meal."

Aaron laughed maniacally, as if to congratulate himself. He continued laughing all the way back to the shore, where I hastily waddled to the nearest restroom, slammed the door, and didn't reemerge for nearly an hour. And when I finally did, that fool was still laughing.

Aaron had to go back to work the next day, so I spent the better part of my time in Florida alone. I found myself falling into many of the same habits that had taken root in Honduras. Most days I either sat in coffee shops reading and writing, or exploring the city on foot. Habitually, life hadn't changed. Aesthetically, it was completely different. I could read the words on signs with complete ease; I understood what people were saying and they understood me; there were gas stations and paved sidewalks in every direction.

When Wednesday—my last full day in Florida—arrived, Aaron asked if I would like to come see the Wednesday night program he put on for his youth group.

"Absolutely," I told him.

Having been heavily involved in my youth group as a teenager, I immediately recognized the format of the evening: the kids played a few games, the band performed some worship songs, Aaron gave a short message, and the band closed out the evening with a few more songs. It was standard, but welcomed.

After church, we went to eat at Chick-fil-A—because that's just what church people do—and I used the opportunity to chat with the students. I told them my story and listened as they told me theirs. They were particularly impressed when I pulled a few Honduran lempiras from my wallet. "It's so crazy!" one girl said, admiring the red bill with a dumbfounded expression, apparently only just having realized that not all countries use U.S. dollars. She nearly lost her mind when I told her she could keep one.

At the end of the evening, Aaron and I drove back to his home alone. "Did you have a good time this week?" he asked.

"Dude, this week was exactly what I needed," I told him. "I

128

know tonight was probably nothing special for you, but it was a breath of fresh air for me."

"I'm glad," he said, parking his car in front of the apartment. "So tell me, how can I be specifically praying for you when you go back?"

"Well..." I said, trailing off. I knew the answer, but I was hesitant to say it. "There's one thing I've been praying for since I got to Honduras, but it hasn't happened yet. I'm scared of saying it out loud, because I don't want to be disappointed if it doesn't happen."

"After everything you've told me this week about your faith," he said, "do you really expect God to give you what you want in the exact way you want it?"

"I guess not," I answered. "Look, this week has been great. I've really needed to have conversations with Americans about life in Honduras. But it's still not enough. I need someone who understands what it's like to be doing what I'm doing. You know, it's one thing to *explain* what life is like, but it would be another thing entirely to have a conversation with someone who can relate—someone in the trenches with me."

"Ok," he said, "so tell me *exactly* how you want me to pray for you."

I sighed. "I want to meet some Americans in Honduras and have an opportunity to debrief."

"Ok," he said. "Then that's what I'll pray for."

I lay in bed that night and stared at the ceiling. In just a few hours, I'd be on an airplane flying southwest, nonstop to Honduras.

Three more months. Halfway done.

It's fine, I assured myself, closing my eyes.

Is it, though? The question crept in from the back of my head.

Yes. I rolled over and pulled the cover to my neck.

Who are you trying to impress? My eyes popped open.

Be honest. Is it fine?

I stared at the wall, its white paint dancing wildly as my eyes adjusted to the darkness. The room was cold—much colder than my bedroom in Oranado would ever be. I thought about the simple pleasure of air conditioning; the assurance of living in a city with constant power; a society of educated individuals to ensure the stability of it all; things Oranado would never know.

I missed this life: cars, cleanliness, familiarity, comfort, English.

No. It's not fine.

I closed my eyes again.

But that's not what this is about.

I now stood on the grassy lot, looking up at Santa Lucia. I saw the faces of my students as they hustled up the stairs to class. I could hear the bell as clearly as if I was standing next to it.

That's what this is about.

I had a duty to fulfill—one bigger than myself. Living in Honduras was hard; being alone was nearly unbearable. Still, I'd committed to teach those kids to the best of my ability.

I wouldn't turn back. No, I would finish. And I would finish strong.

"God," I whispered. "If I'm gonna do this, I'm gonna need some help."

Chapter 18

Round Two

The plane began its final descent over vast fields of coffee and tobacco. In the distance, the mighty mountain slopes stood guard over the southern portion of the country. I was certainly back in Central America. Three months ago, I could hardly contain my giddiness. I'd imagined Honduras as a land full of opportunity, of adventure, of pure and simple fun. How could I have known what was to come?

The excitement was gone. I now knew exactly what awaited me beyond those mountains. I could see the faces so clearly in my mind's eye—of my students, of my colleagues, of Sofía. I was coming back to finish, and finish strong. I had a duty in Oranado and I was determined to see it through.

The plane carried mostly Hispanic passengers with a few gringo faces speckled throughout crowd. I wondered what might have brought them to Honduras. Had they experienced Hispanic culture before? Did they know the dangers of Honduras? Perhaps some were missionaries. Others might have been on business. One or two may have been teachers working in the north part of the country. Would I see any in Copán? Unlikely. The Roatán ferry was no more than an hour north of San Pedro Sula; surely most of these gringos were on their way to a fun-filled tropical Caribbean holiday.

The plane landed, and for the second time in three months, I walked through Honduran Customs. Passing from baggage claim into the wide-open terminal, I immediately began my search for the bus station. José was certain that I'd be able to purchase a bus ticket to Copán in the airport. I just had to find where to start.

I stopped an employee pushing a cart loaded with bags.

"Excuse me. I'm looking for the bus station…"

"*Disculpe?*"

Oh, right. Spanish.

"*Busco a la*…uh…uh… *estación!*…uh yeah, *Busco a la estación de los*, um, *autobuses*."

"*Ah, por supuesto*," he said, offering a few directions and pointing to the glass doors with his head. And with that, he was off again.

"Not bad," I told myself, pulling the straps on my backpack and heading toward the doors.

A small line had formed down a hallway, just short of the main airport entrance. This had to be it. When it came my turn at the window, the young man smiled and, in perfect English, said, "Hello, sir. Where are you traveling to today?"

"Copán Ruinas," I told him.

His fingers rattled the keys of the computer.

"How much for a ticket?" I asked, wincing in preparation.

"Will you be paying with U.S. dollars or Honduran lempiras?" he asked.

"American, I guess," I responded, all too mindful of my dwindling budget. I held my breath, hoping, praying, that I had enough money.

He stroked a few more keys, and then said, "Forty-three dollars, sir."

I audibly exhaled in relief. He must have noticed, but to his credit, didn't say a word. I handed him the folded one hundred dollar bill through the slot.

"Thank you, sir," he said, passing me a ticket atop a small stack of lempiras. "Your bus is scheduled for 3:30. We will begin loading at 3:00."

Two hours to kill. Not a problem, I assured myself. *More time to enjoy the airport.*

I walked to the food court and ordered a frosty at Wendy's, then pulled out my tablet to send José my bus itinerary. Afterwards, I strolled to the gift shop, only then realizing that I hadn't bought a single Honduran souvenir. A barrel full of Honduran flags stared at me from the corner. A flag would do. I offered the cashier a few lempiras and stuffed the flag into my backpack as I left the store. I looked up to the hanging digital clock. 2:30. Half an hour left, and already the small airport had exhausted its entertainment. Making my way back to the hallway, I found an open spot on the floor and took a seat against the wall.

My eyes wandered down the hall as I snuggled my ear buds firmly in place. I recognized two gringos from the plane—a middle-aged man and woman. They stood across the aisle, side by side, holding hands and chatting quietly in one another's ear. We made eye contact for a moment and smiled politely in acknowledgement. I looked down at my tablet to queue up the next song. When I looked up again, the couple still had their eyes on me. Had they said something that I missed?

I pulled one ear bud out and said, "Sorry, what? Uh...*qué?*"

"Oh, pardon me," said the man. "I didn't realize you were listening to music."

English. Awesome.

"It's alright," I answered. "I'm just trying to kill some time before the bus gets here."

"Where are you headed?" the woman asked.

"Copán Ruinas," I said. "It's a little town in the mountains about three hours from here."

Their eyes opened wide and a smile ran across their faces at the same time. "That's where we're going!" said the man.

"Oh, cool!" I said. "You'll like it."

"Have you been there before?" the woman inquired.

"Actually, yes," I said. "It's been my home-away-from-home since January. I was in Florida this week to reset my ninety days in Honduras. I'm coming back to finish up the semester."

The couple seemed intrigued. "Are you a missionary, then?" the man asked.

"Well, no, not really," I said. "I'm a teacher at a little school in a town just down the road from Copán."

"How fantastic!" the woman replied with a full smile.

"What about you guys?" I asked. "What are you doing in Copán?"

"Well," the man said, "Shelly and I sponsor a few kids in Tegucigalpa. We're going to spend three weeks in Copán doing some intensive Spanish classes and then fly down south to meet them."

"Cool," I said, "How much Spanish do you know?"

They looked at one another and laughed. "None," the man said.

"How about you? I'll bet your Spanish is terrific after having lived here for three months."

Now it was my turn to laugh. "Learning another language is a lot harder than I thought it would be. I'm not saying it's impossible. I'm just saying, 'good luck.'"

"We understand that," Shelly said. "David and I both speak French and English."

"Then this might be a walk in the park for you," I said. "If I may ask, why French?"

They looked at one another again, waiting for the other to reply, until finally David said, "We're Canadian."

I tapped my forehead with my palm. "That makes a lot of sense." Before that moment, it hadn't occurred to me that Canadians would have any business in Central America, as if the United States had dibs on everything south of Texas. Suddenly, that idea seemed absurd.

"Well," I said, *"Bienvenidos a Honduras."*

"Gracias!" they said in unison.

The charter bus was larger and more lavish than any I had yet seen in Honduras. The driver maneuvered the gargantuan shuttle through the tiny mountain passes in unbelievable fashion. My new Canadian friends, David and Shelly, sat across the aisle and marveled at the view from the window. We made small talk about life in Honduras as we drove. They asked questions about Copán and the Spanish language and whether I had ever been to Tegucigalpa; I said I hadn't. They told me that they had made one trip before, so they were roughly familiar with Honduran culture.

About thirty minutes before arriving in Copán, the winding roads got the best of me, and I spent the remainder of the drive alone near the back of the bus, trying desperately to keep my frosty from making an encore appearance. American food would surely be the death of me. When we arrived in Copán, the sun was beginning to set. We stepped off the bus and stood on the dusty lot, waiting as the driver unloaded our bags from storage.

"Well," I said, walking toward David and Shelly, "It was good to meet you guys. Good luck in Honduras! I hope your Spanish lessons are useful."

I extended my hand to David, who took it in return. "Thank you, Mark. Good luck to you in your teaching."

I shook Shelly's hand as well, as she wished me the best of luck. Then, finding my backpack, I heaved it over my shoulder and made my way to the exit. Hissela's black Jeep was parallel parked just outside the bus station. José must have filled her in. I tossed my backpack behind the passenger seat and hopped in.

"Welcome back," Hissela said, staring forward. Something was off. She wore her usual smile, but it somehow seemed less defined, as if she were forcing it for a picture. "How was Florida?" she asked.

"It was great," I said, closing the door and buckling my seatbelt. "I definitely needed it."

"I am glad," she answered.

"And now," I added, "we don't have to worry about my ninety days expiring before June."

"Hmm. Yes."

And with that, we were off. Not another word was spoken until we reached Oranado. Hissela drove to the *pulperia* and put the Jeep in park.

"See you at school tomorrow," she said, still staring forward. Something was clearly wrong. But Hissela hadn't seemed to want to talk about it on our ten minute drive from Copán, so I decided to let it be. Surely she would be back to her normal self tomorrow.

I grabbed my backpack and slung it over my shoulder, then walked downstairs to my bedroom and fell atop the bed.

Here we go again. Let's do this.

The world faded into blackness as I fell asleep in my own bed for the first time in over a week.

"MOMMY!" Lora screeched through the courtyard as the sun's first light peeked over the wall.

"*Buenos días*, Lora," I mumbled. "I missed you, too." I threw the covers to the floor and hopped out of bed.

"Finish strong." I repeated my new mantra over and over as I prepared for school.

This shower is freezing.

"Finish strong."

Crap. None of my shirts are clean.

"Finish strong."

It must've rained last night. The road is so muddy.

"Finish strong."

Until at last, there I stood, staring up at the school from the grassy lot. Children poured from the busses as they pulled in from the road. They threw their backpacks over their shoulders and sprinted to the soccer field, hoping to get one good game in before school.

Finish strong.

I scanned the soccer field, spotting my target almost immediately. Making my way across the pavement, I gave Sofía's shoulder a light tap.

"Well, well," I said. "Fancy seeing you here."

Her head turned and a smile crept over her soft face. "Oh, Mr. Mark. It has been so long, I thought you decided to move back to the United States."

"Nope," I said. "I just had some business to take care of."

"Well, did you have a good time?" she asked.

"It was alright," I said. "I can only think of one thing that would have made it better."

"Oh yes?" she replied, lifting an eyebrow. "What is that?"

"If I had a pretty teacher to come with me."

She smiled softly and shrugged. "I am sure Mr. Enrique would have gone with you if you asked him."

I laughed. "Probably. But I was thinking of someone else. Maybe someone who's name starts with an S and sounds like *shmoshía.*"

At that, she broke out into laughter, squinting her eyes. Oh, how I had missed it. Before she could say another word, Hissela took the floor and welcomed the students to school. She showed no signs of anger or sadness. Her smile was at full capacity. Yesterday must have been a fluke, nothing more.

"Mr. Mark is back from the United States," she said, making

sure to speak loud enough that the entire crowd could hear. "So make sure you welcome him back today." A hundred eyes darted back in my direction. Whispers overtook the crowd as the young children pointed and waved, while the middle-schoolers raised their chins. I offered a wave, and Hisslea reclaimed the spotlight.

"Now, this week I would like us to focus on *responsibility*. Who can tell me what that word means?"

No sooner had she started speaking than a hand landed hard on my right shoulder. I turned to see José with his free hand outstretched. "Welcome back, man," he whispered as we shook.

"Thanks, man," I said.

"Did God take care of everything?" he asked.

I laughed quietly and shook my head. "Yeah, he did."

"When are you going to start believing me, man?" he said with a smirk.

"When you learn to speak English," I teased.

He whispered something rapidly in Spanish, then waited for my response.

"Ok, you win," I said, and he laughed.

"Hey man, come to my house tonight," he said. "Let's have dinner again. I want to tell you something important."

"Why can't you tell me now?" I asked. But it was too late. The Honduran National Anthem had already begun. I stood at attention and watched the blue and white flag wave proudly in the wind.

Ah, Honduras. Three more months.

Finish. Strong.

I peered to the side to catch a glimpse of Sofía. She didn't look back; she didn't have to. Her expression said it all.

"It's good to have you back."

PART FOUR

reconnecting

Chapter 19

On Teaching

"Good morning, class," my voice echoed along the cinderblock walls of the sixth grade classroom.

"Good mor-ning, Mee-stair Mark," came the reply in rhythmic unison from sixteen twelve-year-olds.

The chattering came to a halt, with the exception of one or two side comments in Spanish from the right side of the room. I shot a look toward the students and they fell silent.

"Well," I started. "It's good to be back. I missed you all. Did you miss me?"

A mixture of yeses, nos, and laughter emerged from the class.

"Good," I said. "At least I know you're telling the truth." I brought my hands together behind my back and waited for the students to calm down. Luna recognized the gesture and shouted into the chaos, "*Cállese!*" Not my preferred method for regaining the class's attention, but it was effective. The room grew quiet.

"I've been gone for a while," I began again. "So I know you have some stories for me." The class sat in silence. "Oh, come on, guys. Somebody had to have done *something*. It's almost been a whole week!"

It had become routine to begin the sixth grade Reading by opening the floor for stories from the night before. Responses were rare, but occasionally a student decided to speak up. If they didn't, I did my best to come up with a story. It ate into class time a bit, but I knew that nearly every student would leave school and sit in front of a television set for the remainder of the evening. If storytelling inspired my students to get out of the house and do something, then the lost class time was worth it. Besides, it allowed for some good English practice.

"Well, if no one did anything this week, I've got some stories to tell," I announced.

A hand shot up on the left side of the room. "Yes, Diego?" I said.

141

"Did you go to Miami, Mee-stair?"

"Good question," I said. "I didn't go to Miami, but I did go to Florida. Miami is part of Florida."

"Ah, yes," he said. "But why did you go to the U.S., Mee-stair?"

"Well, I had to leave Honduras for three days," I explained. "I was going to get into trouble with the government."

Another hand lifted. "Gabriel?" I called.

"My uncle was in trouble once with the government," he said. "He had to go to jail, and when he was free, he breaked his leg from a car crash."

"My uncle likes to smoke marijuana!" a voice from across the room interjected.

"Juan," I said firmly, looking directly into his eyes as his smile faded and his face slumped downward. "Maybe you would like to be in trouble yourself?"

Juan shook his head, still looking at me. "No, Mee-stair," he said. "I am sorry."

"One more outburst like that and you're leaving the room. Do you understand?" I asked.

"Yes, Mee-stair," came his somber reply.

Even after three months, it felt odd being forced to exercise my power over the class. I was twenty-five years old. I didn't even have a bachelor's degree. Before coming to Honduras, I never quite felt like an adult. Now, with only a few words and one or two facial expressions, I was able to command complete control and submission of an entire classroom.

"What were you saying, Gabriel?" I said, hoping to bring the conversation back.

"Oh, nothing Mee-stair," he said with a shrug, as if he'd already forgotten his story. Nobody seemed to care, and nobody ever brought it up again. Kids are weird sometimes.

Sixth grade was made up of mostly girls; the biggest problem I faced in that class was sass. Seventh grade was mostly boys. Their biggest problem: rowdiness. As soon as one teacher left, the classroom erupted into disarray. I left sixth grade and walked to the open door leading to seventh. For a moment, I just watched. Students stood over one another's desks, each voice struggling to overpower the others. In the corner, four boys wadded sheets of paper into balls and practiced their free-throw techniques into a trashcan. At the opposite end, two boys with plastic rulers had started to sword fight.

Chaos.

I think in a billion years, when the sun starts to run out of energy, we should connect wires to giant hamster wheels and make middle-school boys run on them. Energy will never be a problem again.

As soon as I entered the room, I was overwhelmed by cries of "HEY! MEE-STAIR MARK! HOW ARE YOU DOING!? WE MISSED YOU! WHAT'S UP?" It was welcoming, to be sure, but I was all too aware that if I didn't take control immediately, anarchy would rule the day.

"Sit down, guys," I said calmly, trying my hardest not to crack a smile. Teachers have a great social disadvantage; I found that the students I was forced to punish most often were my favorite. "Hey! What did I just say?"

The students found their seats and conversations began to taper off. Unlike sixth grade, I was always one eggshell away from losing my seventh-graders for the remainder of class. I wasn't able to open up the floor for stories, but if they promised to behave, I often allowed them to work in groups. They seemed to get more done that way anyway.

"Well guys," I said. "It's Reading class. Did you read any further in *Holes* while I was gone?"

"Yes, Mee-stair!" came a piercing shout from the back of the room.

"I'm sorry, Dante. Were you saying something?" I asked.

"Oh, yes. Sorry, mee-stair," came the reply. He then put his hand into the air.

"Yes, Dante," I said, trying not to roll my eyes.

"We read a little bit," he said, using his finger and thumb to demonstrate.

"Please do not make us have a quiz!" another voice shouted from

143

the left side of the room.

I placed my hands on my hips and turned my head. "Did you have something *you* wanted to say, Luis?"

He looked at me with a blank stare. "No, Mee-stair. I have nothing to say," he said.

I choked back a laugh. Kids are so weird.

"Well, it's Friday," I told the class. "We can try to read as much as possible and finish the rest for homework this weekend..." My proposal was met with groans and shaking heads in every direction. "BUT," I interjected, bringing the whines to a halt, "I've been gone all week and I didn't actually plan anything for today, so if you're ok with it, maybe we can just skip the reading today and not have any homework this weekend." No sooner had the words left my mouth than the class burst into a roaring applause. Using my hands, I calmed the cheers and added, "But you have to promise to behave. I can still assign homework."

"No, Mee-stair. We will be good," I heard from multiple voices throughout the room.

A hand darted into the air from the front row. "Yes, Rico?"

"You can tell us about your week in Miami," he suggested.

I shook my head. "Not Miami."

He shrugged.

"Do you guys want to hear about my week?" I asked.

A chorus of yeses emerged from the students.

"Well," I began, but was quickly interrupted by a girl on the back row.

"But Mee-stair," Camila said, "you should tell us the story in Spanish."

I fought back a smile, but it was no use. "Do you guys want to hear my story in Spanish?" I asked.

The students nodded and laughed. A good show was on the way.

"Do you promise not to make fun of me?" I leaned back against the desk at the front of the room.

"Yes, we promise," Dante said.

I looked down and gave a sigh. "Ok, here goes," I said, clearing my throat. I then proceeded to tell as much of my story in Spanish that I possibly could. It was littered with grammatical mistakes, and interrupted far too often with "*Cómo se dice* this or that," both of which sent the class into fits of laughter. Normally I would try to bring it back, but that day was different. That day I was the student.

Eighth grade was a completely different beast. These were the oldest students in the school—two girls and two boys. During my first few days of teaching, I assumed that this would be the easiest grade to teach. Oh, how wrong I was.

The girls were exceptional in their English, which brought a good amount of arrogance with it. More than a few times, they simply decided not to do their homework, because "We do not need to learn these things. We already know." The boys, on the other hand, had little respect for authority, much less a dumb gringo with barely any understanding of their native tongue.

"Hey guys," I said, entering the small room for the first time in a week.

"Hey, what's up, Mee-stair?" replied Sara, sitting backwards in her chair watching as Martín drew a picture on a sheet of notebook paper. "How was Miami?"

I dropped my backpack onto the front desk. "You guys know that there's more in the U.S. than Miami, right?"

Sara kept her stare toward the paper.

"What are you drawing there, Martín?" I asked.

His head remained downward, focused intently on his masterpiece.

"Martín," I tried again. "Martín!"

His head shot up to meet my eyes. "What, Mee-stair?"

I shook my head. Kids are weird.

"Do you guys have homework in other classes?"

All four students nodded.

"What if we use class today to get caught up on homework?" I offered.

"Yes, Mee-stair," replied Abril. "That would be very good for me."

Martín continued his artwork as Sara marveled at it. Abril pulled out a notebook and got to work solving math problems. Rodrigo sat in his seat staring forward, deep in thought—or possibly not thinking at all.

"Do you guys want to hear about my trip?" I offered.

Not one student responded. "Fair enough," I said, leaning back in my chair.

Being a teacher taught me a lot of things I never would have learned otherwise, most importantly, that I don't want to be a teacher—at least, not like that. I'd be willing to work with students, even in a classroom setting, but teaching full classes was the hardest job I'd ever had. It wasn't that I didn't like my students. On the contrary, liking my students is what made the job so hard.

It takes a special kind of person to be a teacher. They have to have a genuine affection for their students, but still be able to put aside that affection for the sake of the class. If a teacher leans too far one way or the other, problems occur.

During my practicum that Fall, I'd worked under a teacher who hated kids. I know this because it was the first sentence out of her mouth every day after dropping the students off for lunch. "I hate kids," she would mutter, walking away from the crowded cafeteria, wiping her hands on her jeans as if to cleanse herself of the filth. She needn't have said anything, though. It was obvious. Her disdain for children showed in the militant way she ran her classroom. No one was allowed to speak, stand up, or breathe without a public scolding and an office referral. As such, her students hated her in return.

On the other hand, I'd seen teachers lose control of their classroom because they were more inclined to treat their students as friends rather than subordinates. It's a great idea in theory: *If I can just* earn *these students' respect, I won't* have *to punish them.* But those students, they're crafty. They spend the first few weeks pushing the limits, and they learn exactly how far they can go before trouble ensues. Once that line is established, it becomes the law for the rest of the semester.

I'm the second type of teacher.

I've always enjoyed working with young people. They have an energy that adults lose somewhere in their teenage years and don't generally find again. Because of this, I find that I spend more time with young people than I do with those my age or older. I had learned how to command respect from my students over the months, but it always tore my heart a little when I did.

The first time I realized how much of an impact it had on me, I was teaching sixth-grade History class. We had just started a new unit on Africa. The first assignment was a simple one: draw a rough map of Africa and color it in by geographical regions. I'd given my students two days to complete the task, and the time had come to check their work. Being a relatively easy assignment, I decided to grade on completion only. Walking around the room, I checked each student's map and jotted down a note in my grade book. Two students sitting side-by-side, Ángel and Lorenzo, sat digging through their backpacks and asked if I would come back after they found their maps. I moved on, quickly checking and marking. When I reached the end, I heard Lorenzo call from across the room.

"Mee-stair Mark, I find my map!"

I walked back to his desk as he presented me with a sheet of paper torn around the edges. It was sloppy, but the map was complete and his name was written at the top. Sometimes it was better not to question Lorenzo's actions. He had a habit of staring blankly and saying, "What, Mee-stair?"

I jotted a completion score in my book and looked toward Ángel. "Did you find yours?" I asked.

"No, Mee-stair, not yet," he said. "I continue to look."

I placed my grade book on the front desk and called the attention of the students.

"Alright, guys, who can tell me something about the Sahara Desert?"

A few hands went up. I glanced around the room and landed on Ángel's desk. He was tearing the edges from a sheet of paper. Curious, I crossed the room, just as Lorenzo began swatting at Ángel's hands and frantically whispering in Spanish.

"What are you doing, Ángel?" I asked. His head darted up. In an

147

instant, the paper was beneath his desk.

"Me? No. Nothing. I do nothing, Mee-stair."

"May I see that paper you're holding?" I asked.

Ángel sat in silence for a moment. Then, accepting his defeat, he passed the sheet to my outstretched hand and hung his head downward. I held the page before me, suddenly connecting the dots. In my hand, I held the completed map of another student. Ángel had been tearing off the edges, and with them, the student's name.

My eyes moved from the map to Ángel to Lorenzo. The boys knew they had been caught red-handed. I sighed, and then, knowing what had to be done, said, "Come with me, boys."

The boys followed me outside to the cafeteria, heads hung low. They each took a seat on the bench. I sat down opposite from them and searched for the words.

"Do you understand that you're in trouble?" I finally asked, very quietly.

The boys both nodded, refusing to make eye contact.

"Do you understand *why* you're in trouble?" I asked.

This time they simply stared at the ground as their eyes glossed over with tears.

"Have you ever heard the word *plagiarism*?" I asked.

Both heads shook slowly.

"Plagiarism is when you take somebody else's work and you tell people that it's yours," I explained. "It's when you lie about what you did. It can get you into a lot of trouble."

One by one their teardrops began to fall to the ground. I hated what I had to do next, but I knew it had to be done.

"I have to send you guys to the office," I said. "You both know that we practice honesty in this school. What you did wasn't honest. You cheated and then you lied about it."

The boys slowly stood to their feet and quietly walked to the office, tears streaming. Now that they were gone, I could let my guard down. I exhaled deeply and lowered my forehead into my palms. My hands shook with anxiety. I was worried, but unable to pinpoint what exactly it was that worried me. I thought about my child-hating practicum teacher. Had she been in my shoes, she would have rolled her eyes, stuck up her chin, and said, "I hope they get what they deserve." But that wasn't me.

I stood to my feet and paced around the small cafeteria, trying to shake the feeling, but still it lingered. Was it possible that it was growing? The more I dwelt on it, the more I began to understand that I was worried for the two boys. I didn't want to see them punished. What would happen at home when their parents found out? How must they be feeling right now?

This is stupid. You're a teacher. You don't have to worry about this, I told myself. *Crime and punishment. This is a learning experience for them.* But as much as I knew those things were true, I still couldn't calm myself down. I walked back into the sixth grade classroom and wiped the sweat from my head.

The room was silent. Every face stared solemnly at me. "Let's all get out our books and turn to page seventy-one," I said to the class. Everyone obeyed.

Sixth grade History was followed by my free period. I walked back to the cafeteria, passing the boys just as they left the office. They looked up to avoid running into the oncoming adult, but seeing who it was, their bloodshot eyes darted down to the sidewalk again.

I came to a halt and turned my head to follow them into the room. *I really like those guys*, I thought. *I hate that they're settling for less than what they're capable of.*

And suddenly, it clicked; I knew why I had experienced such anxiety. I was feeling *for* them. I had taken the weight of being caught in a lie, of being sent to the office, of disappointing the teacher, of facing my parents in a few short hours, and of trying to get along until then. These weren't bad kids; they were *my* kids.

Every one of my students had personalities and quirks that made them unique and likeable for different reasons. Sure, some of them caused trouble from time to time, but their poor choices didn't define them as people—people that I really liked. Watching them punished— and worse, being the punisher—took an emotional toll.

Teaching is one of the hardest jobs in the world. Not everyone is cut out for it, and that includes a lot of professional teachers. However, those who are good at it are usually the most phenomenal people you're likely to meet. We should really consider paying them what they deserve.

Chapter 20

Sacrifice

"How's it going, man?"

José sat on the top step leading to his front door. Earlier that day, he had invited me to dinner in order to share some "important" news. I couldn't begin to guess what it might be, but José was one of the most optimistic people I knew. I assumed it must be something good.

"What happened to the pig?" I asked, pointing to the house next door.

José shrugged. "I guess they got hungry."

I shook my head and snickered. "This place."

"Oh yes," José said. "I forgot that no one in the U.S. eats bacon or pork chops."

"Fair," I said. "So, what's for dinner here?"

"Spaghetti," he said. While it wouldn't be the first time I'd eaten spaghetti in Honduras, I was still surprised. *Spaghetti is an American dish, don't you know? I mean, sure, it's Italian, but it belongs to us, because…'Murca.*

"Sounds good." I was close enough to see straight through the open doorway into the small house where José's little daughter, Claudia, stood behind the wall, shielding half her face as she watched us speak. I bent down and stretched my hand out to wave. *"Hola, Claudia."* She said nothing, but giggled at the gesture.

José turned around. *"Me saludas a Mr. Mark,"* he said.

"Hola," her soft, muffled voice crept from behind the wall.

José gave a proud smile and turned back to me. "Are you hungry, man?" he asked.

"I'm always hungry in this country. My friends aren't going to recognize me when I get back. I look like a twig."

"Come inside. Let's eat."

We made our way inside and sat down at the table. Soon, we

151

were greeted with a bowl of spaghetti and a plate stacked with corn tortillas. "*Gracias, amor*," José said to Anahí, his wife, as she walked back into the kitchen to fetch drinks.

"Alright," I said. "I can't wait anymore. What's this big news?"

He laughed. "I did not think you would remember."

"Oh, I remembered," I shot back. "You can't just tell someone that you've got big news in the morning and leave them hanging until night. It'll drive a person crazy."

Anahí reappeared with three glasses of water and set them on the table, then sat down and scooped a small portion of spaghetti onto Claudia's plate.

"Sometimes crazy is the best," José said, smiling. He seemed giddy.

"Ok, crazy man," I said. "Tell me your news."

"You might think I *am* crazy when I tell you," he answered.

"José! Tell me!"

His smile stretched from one ear to the other. He placed one hand on my shoulder and then looked deep into my eyes. "I am going to the U.S."

"What?!"

He burst into a fit of laughter and clapped his hands together wildly. Claudia giggled furiously at her father. Even Anahí, who couldn't understand a word of our conversation, fought to keep her food from falling out of her mouth through the smile on her face.

"That's awesome!" I said. "When? Where? Wait...start over! What?!"

"I have been thinking about this for a long time," he told me. "I keep praying to God to help me provide for my family. I want my daughter to have a good life with many opportunities. I must pay off my debt and I must help her go to university. So I am going to go work in the U.S. for five years and then return to Honduras to be with my family."

"That sounds great," I said, sincerely. "So how are you getting to the States?"

"Well, that is the crazy part," His smile faded slightly. "I must take a bus to Mexico and come to the border of Texas. Then we will go into the U.S. in secret. I have friends in Mary—how do you say...Maryland?—who can help for me to get a job."

My smile had vanished. I was speechless. José's plan was to be smuggled across the border and try to get all the way to Maryland to work illegally for five years. It was not an impossible task, but the odds were slim. I wanted to share the joy that José felt at that moment. I just couldn't bring myself to believe that he would succeed.

"What do you think, man?" he said after a few seconds of contemplative silence.

"José, listen. You're right. This is crazy. I want this for you, but I don't think it's going to work. Have you tried *everything* else? Have you talked to anyone about this?"

He reached out to the chair on his right where Claudia sat, playing with her spaghetti noodles. He lifted her tiny body and set her down on his lap. "My family is worth the risk," he said, bouncing her on one knee. "Listen, man, my father told me something when I was very young: 'Without sacrifice there is no victory.' If I am caught at the border, then God will take care of me and my family in a different way. I must try, though."

I hung my head and shrugged. "If you're sure about this, then I'll support you. I really want this for you. Do you believe me?"

"Of course," he said.

"I just don't think it's going to work like you hope it will." Then I added. "... I'm sorry."

"Do not worry, man," José said. "God is going to take care of everything."

"I hope so," I said.

"I know so," José responded, setting Claudia back in her chair and taking a huge bite out of a folded tortilla.

Chapter 21

El Salto

It wasn't long before I made another trip to José's house, but this time for a completely different reason.

"You own an electric razor, right?" I asked.

"Yeah...?"

"Wanna shave my head?"

There was no reason for it. I knew I'd probably look like an idiot. Still, I wanted to do something I had never done before.

José agreed to do the deed, although he made it no secret that he thought this was the worst idea any gringo ever had. Turns out he was right. I made a trip to the market later that day and bought two hats.

On my first day as a bald teacher, I received horrified looks from the entire student body. The teachers tried to be respectful, but even they had difficulty not staring in shock for too long. Hissela passed my between classes, rolled her eyes, and kept walking without a word.

"You should return to the barber shop and tell them to put it back on," Enrique told me.

"José did it," I said.

"Well, I hope you did not pay him too much money." He said, laughing at his own joke.

I laughed too. So what if I looked terrible? It would grow back soon enough. The point was never to improve my physique. I simply wanted to try something I was unsure of. If I hadn't shaved my head that day, I probably never would have.

"So when do you want to go hiking again?" Enrique asked.

I laughed even harder at that. "Enrique, your version of hiking is what most people call *cruel and unusual punishment*."

He waved off the comment and rolled his eyes. "Come on," he said. "You told me that there are no mountains where you live. You love mountains, right? You should enjoy them while you can." He was right, even if I didn't want to admit it. I remained silent and gave him a look

155

that said *I'm not convinced... but I could be.* "What if we take a small hike after school?" he suggested.

I sighed dramatically. "Fine. I guess that would be ok."

We planned the hike for the next day. Enrique had some errands to run after school, so I would have to wait about an hour before we could head out. We would meet at the bus stop and take the road up the mountain to Alta Vista, a tiny town situated at the peak. About twenty students in Santa Lucia lived in Alta Vista. We would meet up with them and spend a few hours exploring the town.

José soon joined the conversation and expressed his interest in the hike.

"Come with us," I said.

José needed no further convincing.

Later that day, Sofía told me that she too was looking forward to the hike. Apparently José and Enrique had told her that I refused to go unless she joined. "Thanks, friends," I told them later. They just giggled like schoolgirls.

The students were especially excited for our arrival. "Wear clothes that you can get wet," I was told.

The final bell rang, signaling the end of the school day. Kids and adults poured from the classrooms and made their way to their respective busses. I waded through the current of students to the grassy lot. There I waited until I saw Sofía coming down the steps. Once she arrived, we began the walk into town together. "I'm going to run home and change my clothes," I told her. "I'll meet you in front of the supermarket."

When we reached the bottom of the hill, I took off in a sprint toward home. I threw on a pair of trunks and my new Barcelona soccer jersey, then snagged a hat on my way out the door.

I arrived at the supermarket dripping with sweat and completely out of breath. Sofía smiled. "You did not have to run so fast," she said. "We have an hour before Enrique is finished."

"Well, yeah," I said, gasping for air, "but I can't just leave a pretty lady out here alone. This country is dangerous, you know."

She smiled. "I am much safer in Honduras than you are, Mark."

I took a seat next to her on the concrete steps. "Where's your daughter?" I asked.

"My mother is taking care of her until I get back tonight," she said.

"Isn't your fiancé home?" I asked.

"Oh no," she said calmly. "I do not know what he is doing."

"Cool," I shrugged. "You guys meeting up later then?"

"No."

"No?"

"No," she repeated with a scowl. "And I hope I never see that... that *pendejo* again."

"Um..." I eased in. "Is everything...you know...ok?"

"Yes, everything is ok," she said, blinking rapidly and turning to face me. "Everything is better now. I do not need him."

"Sofía, you're about the closest thing I have to a best friend in this country. You don't have to tell me anything you don't want to, but I'd be lying if I said I'm not curious."

She closed her eyes and sighed. "He is a liar. *A liar!* First, he does not tell me that he has three children. We lived together for two months before I found out. And he always treats me like property. I tell him, 'I am your *novia*, not your dog.' But still, he does not care."

"Wow, I'm sor..."

"*And*," she cut me off. "he always leaves. Always! I ask, 'Where are you going?' But he never answers. Then I see his phone and I learn that he is sleeping with a girl in Guatemala. He has been cheating on me for longer than I have known him!"

I was shocked. This was all news to me. We sat in silence for a moment, her eyes fixed to the ground. "You know," I finally said, "you could have told me yesterday. I don't want you to feel forced to hang out if you need time alone. I know how important..."

"No," she interrupted, shaking her head as if to pull herself from a trance. "I learned this a few weeks ago. I am fine now."

"You sure?"

She looked at me and forced a smile. "I like spending time with you, Mark. Let's have fun today."

Our conversation evolved to work, and from there to my time in

Florida. I told her about the greasy burger that almost caused me to jump into shark-infested water. She let out an adorable laugh that got me laughing, which made her laugh even harder. Talking to Sofía was so easy and so fun. It was a shame we would never be more than friends.

It wasn't as if I hadn't thought about it; I had, every day for three months. Now she was single. The threat of her ambiguous fiancé learning of our flirt-filled free periods no longer hovered over our shared cafeteria table. I finally had a chance with Sofía that I never thought would come.

And yet, I would never take it. For all of Sofía's wonderful qualities, one would forever keep me at arm's length: her daughter. I was nowhere near ready to take on the responsibilities of a father. But more than that, I was trapped in the snare of a stigma with roots as deep as my very soul—one that required a marriage before the birth of a child.

Sofía was just a friend—a gorgeous friend, smart and funny, with every quality that makes a girl so easy to like—but still, just a friend.

Enrique and José arrived not long after, and we began our ascent up the dirt road, talking sparsely to conserve energy. Thirty minutes up, we stopped to admire the view. Far below in the valley rested Oranado. From there it looked like a model town in a Christmas decoration. Oranado wouldn't be seeing snow any time soon, though. Further and further up we hiked, always following the dirt road before us. There came a stretch where the incline leveled out for a few hundred yards. Off the road and across the grassy plane, a handful of children were playing soccer. Just beyond their makeshift soccer field, the cliff dropped off, presenting a magnificent backdrop.

I stopped for a moment, causing Sofía and José to nearly fall over behind me.

"Is everything ok, man?" José asked.

Enrique turned around to look.

"I just think that's cool," I said, staring at the soccer game with a smile. "You know, just playing soccer on top of a mountain like that. I wonder what they would do if someone kicked the ball over the edge."

"Only a gringo would do something like that," Enrique said. Sofía laughed.

At that, we started back up the mountain.

We had walked for nearly an hour when the road took a sharp turn around a hedge of pine trees and gently sloped downward. Beyond the trees, we arrived in a small town of fenced-in concrete homes and a few small shops. On the hilltop sat a church. Children rode bicycles through the streets while men carried bundles of sticks into the gated yards.

"*Estamos aquí!*" Enrique shouted victoriously. "We are here!"

A young girl bolted from one of the shops and shouted "*Están aquí! Están aquí!*" I recognized her as soon as she had spoken: Vanessa from sixth grade. She ran up the slope as more and more children emerged from their homes in groups of two or three to meet us at the edge of town. I recognized most of them from school, but a few faces were unfamiliar.

The Hondurans spoke quickly with one another, making it hard to keep up. Suddenly, the small group turned around and began making its way back down the road into the small town. "Come on, Mee-stair!" said Dante, a seventh grader. "We must go to *el salto!*"

"What's *el salto*?" I asked.

"It is the...the..." He rubbed his hands together and squinted his eyes, searching desperately for the right word. "The JUMP!" he exclaimed.

"And what's 'the jump'?" I asked warily.

"Come, Mee-stair, you will see!" With that, he skipped down the road and caught up with the crowd.

I followed closely behind the group of children as they guided us through town. Before long, the road was surrounded on either side with huge pine trees. We were definitely headed down the backside of the mountain now. The children pointed to a section in the barbed wire fence where the wire was bent just enough to crawl through. One by one we wriggled our bodies through the hole and kept along the footpath through the woods.

As we continued down, the sound of rushing water grew louder and louder, but without any visible source. A large crack in the ground ran only a few feet from the trail. I stepped out from the line of hikers to get a peek. Inside the crack was a steep canyon with a river running at its base.

"Dante!" I called back to the group. "What is this?"

He left his place in line and scurried to my side. "This is where we must go!" he said, barely able to contain his excitement.

"This is *el salto*?"

"No, Mee-stair. Just come!" And with that, he jumped back in line.

The sloping trail finally emerged from the trees into a meadow of smooth rock, separated into two halves by the narrow river that fed from the crevice, disappearing on the far side of the forest. The boys took off their t-shirts and threw them to the ground while a pile of shoes and socks soon formed on the rocky surface. The younger children began to wade in the pool at the end of the current. They were careful to keep to the edge of the water, as the riverbed, though not wide, quickly sloped to a dangerous depth beneath them.

I followed a group of boys back up to the edge of the crevice. Planting my feet firmly on the rock, I leaned over to glance at the rushing water below. Nearly twenty feet stood between our toes and the deep green current below that splashed onto the narrow walls on either side, with a mere six feet separating the sides of sharp, broken rock walls.

"Jump, Mee-stair!" Dante's voice called from behind me.

I turned my head back with a bewildered look. "You're crazy if you think I'm jumping down there!"

A small body came hurtling through the group. "Move, Mee-stair!" Manuel shouted, pushing me to the side. Then, without a second thought, his feet leapt from the smooth edge and his body fell between the canyon walls, causing a giant splash as he disappeared completely beneath the water. All the children laughed and cheered. Excited chatter broke out in every direction. One by one the boys took turns jumping from the cliff into the river below. One particularly eager boy wasted no time in waiting for the previous jumper to swim out of the way. He dove headlong into the canyon and barely missed his amigo treading water by inches. Two heads emerged from the surface and the boys splashed each other in retribution.

160

When my turn finally came, I froze. All eyes were on me, including Sofía's.

"Ok!" I said loudly. "One...two..."

Deep breath, deep breath.

"Three!"

My feet were frozen to the ground. I took another breath and closed my eyes tightly. "I'M SO FRICKIN' SCARED RIGHT NOW!" I shouted at the top of my lungs. That was all it took to drive out the panic. Opening my eyes, I looked at my target below and hurled my body into the narrow canyon, screaming all the way down.

My head broke the cold surface, greeted by wild applause and laughter. I swam the length of the river and came out into the pool with the children. "That was awesome!" I exclaimed. "I gotta do that again!"

Over the next thirty minutes, we took turns cliff jumping, trying more creative and hilarious methods with each jump. Standing in line on the smooth ground, I felt a tug on my jersey. "Come, Mee-stair," Dante said. "We will go see the *cascada*."

"What does that mean?" I asked.

"Waterfall," Enrique's voice interjected from behind.

"Sweet!" I said, following Dante as he led me back toward the woods. Enrique trailed closely behind.

Just past the tree line, the ground split, creating a crevasse that led down into the river canyon. We climbed down until we reached the water. A few trees had fallen into the canyon, creating natural bridges over the water. For the most part, though, we were forced to wade through the waist-deep river, pushing against the current. The narrow walls slithered through the earth, twisting back and forth. The farther we pushed into the canyon, the taller the walls grew. At the top, green moss blanketed the smooth surface of the rocks. Water dripped from the greenery down the damp, curvy surface of the steep walls. Tree branches high above came together in a leafy canopy and shaded the deep trench from the sun.

At last, the thin hallway opened up to reveal a wide chamber full of water. The walls were even higher here than they had yet been. The treetops above seemed miles away. There was not a dry inch in this natural cathedral. At its most shallow point, the water came to my naval.

161

Across the pool, a twenty-foot waterfall poured over a low cliff and slammed through the surface below, commanding the attention of all who dared trek this far.

"Dante!" I shouted above the echoing roar against the cavern walls, "This is incredible!"

Dante just smiled. Enrique stood in the water, with his hands on his hips, admiring the scenery. And there we stayed—five minutes? Ten? Time had no relevance. There was something sacred about this place— like God had invited us into his private sculpting room to show us his masterpiece.

We retraced our steps through the canyon without a word. When we emerged onto the rocky meadow, Dante ran to the edge of the cliff and jumped in. Enrique walked to the kiddy pool and splashed his feet. I watched for a moment, then took a seat right where I was.

A game of tag had broken out across the way. Two young girls ran my direction screaming. One ducked behind my back, using my shoulders for balance. "*Ayudame*, Mee-stair!" she screamed through her unrestrained laughter. "Help!" She darted back toward the kiddy pool, trailed by her friend.

"Mee-stair, look me!"

I turned to find the voice. Franco waved his hands high above his head, with his back toward the crevice. The moment he had my attention, he lunged backwards, falling into the canyon with flailing arms. The surrounding boys laughed hysterically, looking to see my reaction. I shook my head with a smile.

"You guys are crazy!" I called.

Sofía, dangling her feet over the canyon, turned to me and smiled. José wandered to my side and sat down. "I am glad we did this, man," he commented.

I nodded. "Me too, man."

This was good. This was right.

I was exactly where I was supposed to be. I knew it.

For one beautiful afternoon, I was as Honduran as everyone else on that mountain.

"I think I'm gonna make it, José" I said. "I really am gonna finish strong."

Chapter 22

Panhandling

I'd passed the sign for *Canopy Tours* countless times on my weekend walks through Copán. It sat about a mile outside of town, just past the Mayatan Bilingual School, directing passersby to a tin awning a few feet off the road. On its beams hung helmets, pulleys, harnesses, and ropes. It was a tourist trap, to be sure. But with good reason: who doesn't love a good zip line?

Of course, something so blatantly aimed at international tourists was bound to be expensive. Still, I could only breeze by so many times before temptation seized me. I *had* to give it a try. I was doing ok financially, even in spite of Santa Lucia. Paychecks were miniscule (the few times I actually received them), but I kept afloat; a fairly decent federal tax return had come in a few weeks prior, which Mom and Dad deposited into my bank account. When money started running low, I made a trip to the ATM in Copán and lived off of it for as long as I could.

My wallet was full the day I decided to try the zip line. I marched through Copán, up the hill, across the bridge, past the *Canopy Tours* sign, and straight to the awning. Two men sitting in the shade stood to greet me in Spanish. I asked how much a zip line tour would cost.

"*Novecientos.*"

I whistled. Nine hundred lempiras was more than I had spent on anything in Honduras (with the exception of my plane ticket to Florida). *When will I ever have this opportunity again?* I thought, pulling my wallet from my back pocket and counting the cash inside. Nine hundred and twenty lempiras. If I zip lined now, I would have twenty left. *It's fine*, I told myself. *I'll just have to make sure I hit the ATM before going back to Oranado.* Placing the remaining twenty back between the fold, I handed the stack of cash to the man. He counted and smiled.

"*Vámanos!*"

In no time, I had a harness around my waist and thick gloves on my hands. Apparently the helmets were only for decoration. We hopped in the bed of a red pickup truck and were soon scaling the unkempt road up the mountain. The guide explained the procedure of speeding up, slowing down, and watching for hand signals. Afterwards, he asked where I was from and what I was doing in Honduras. I told him the short version of my story, stumbling through in Spanish. He asked whether I liked the idea of zipping at full speed. "*Sí!*" I said. "*Excelente,*" he replied, giving me a thumbs-up.

A sample zip line was set up between two trees at the peak. The men allowed me to practice braking with my hands a few times and then decided I was ready. The first line was nothing impressive. It hung only a few feet from the ground and ran fifty yards or so. The second, however, spanned hundreds of feet straight across a huge ravine. Were my pulley to break or the cable to snap, I would have been dead in seconds. My guide gave me the "go" signal and I leapt as far as I possibly could over certain death. The pulley caught the line and soared across at lightning speed. It was absolutely exhilarating. I looked down and watched my feet glide above the treetops below. The mountains stood tall in every direction, moving aside to reveal even more as I flew from one treetop to the next. Ahead, my guide stood on the wooden platform, giving hand signals. I pulled down on the cable with all my might and slowed to a crawl as he grew closer and closer, finally coming to a complete stop just before he reached out and pulled me to the platform.

"*Buen trabajo, amigo!*" he complimented.

"That was awesome!" I said. "How many more...um...*cuántos más antes de,* uh, *de la tierra?*"

"*Catorce,*" he answered with a grin. *Fourteen.*

This was worth every single lempira.

When at last we reached the base, I removed my harness and gloves, thanking the two men over and over. They were more than happy to show a tourist a good time—and make a considerable living while doing it. One man asked if I would like a ride back to town. I accepted the offer and hopped back into the truck bed.

We made it just after 3:00. I still had two hours before the last bus to Oranado rolled out for the day. Slipping my earbuds in, I made my way down the cobblestone streets of Copán. I passed the tents where the women sold handmade jewelry and rounded the corner at the hardware store, finally arriving at my destination: the best coffee shop in Copán Ruinas, *Café San Rafael*. Honduras boasts the best coffee in the world, and the locals boast the best coffee in Honduras. *Café San Rafael* was easily my favorite coffee in town, so if the claims were true, then I'd spent my weekends drinking the best cup of coffee on planet earth, and I wouldn't argue the matter.

A green wall overgrown with ivy surrounded the small restaurant. I walked through the door, propped wide open, and went straight to the counter. The barista recognized me and offered a quick nod.

"*Café negro hoy?*" he asked. I nodded and handed over my last twenty. He poured a fresh, steaming cup of coffee and passed it over the counter.

"*Gracias*," I said.

I took the coffee and made my way further into the covered courtyard to find a seat. That's when I heard my name.

"Mark?" a female voice called tentatively. I pulled one earbud out and turned around. At the table I'd just passed sat my two Canadian friends, David and Shelly. An older Hispanic lady sat between them with an open book.

"Mark!" Shelly exclaimed. "How have you been?"

"I like your new hairdo," David said.

I laughed. "Thanks. It was an impulse decision. You guys have been here a few weeks now, right? How's Honduras treating you?"

"It's great!," Shelly answered. "We've got a couple more days in Copán and then we're flying out to Tegucigalpa."

"Great," I said. "How's the Spanish coming along?"

David turned to the lady at the table, then back to me. "We're getting there. This is Carmen, our teacher."

"*Mucho gusto*," I said, offering a quick wave. She returned the gesture with a polite smile and a nod.

"Well," David spoke up after a brief pause, "I guess we'll let you go drink your coffee."

"Thanks, guys," I said. "Good luck." I started off toward an open table in the back, when I heard Shelly's voice again. "Hey Mark!"

I spun back around. Shelly was organizing some papers on the table. She pushed her chair out and stood up. "Why don't we get together some time for dinner before we leave?" David nodded in agreement from his seat.

"Ok," I said. "That sounds great."

"When are you free in the next couple days?" she asked.

I thought for a moment. "I could do Monday after school, if that works for you."

Shelly looked down to David who gave a shrug and nodded. "Monday it is!" she said. We exchanged email addresses and said our goodbyes for the day.

Making my way to the table in the corner, I dropped my backpack and began to unload it. A Bible, spiral notebook, tablet, and pen all spread across the table, creating a private arena for my thoughts. Scooping a spoonful of raw, brown crystals from the sugar jar in the center, I dumped it into my black coffee and stirred it with a spoon.

Starbucks was forever ruined.

An hour and a half passed. It would be 5:00 soon; time to wrap things up and get to the bus. I opened the center flap of my backpack, placing my notebook and Bible gently inside. As I sat hunched over in my chair, I heard the familiar ringing of an incoming call through my earbuds. I sat up and looked at the screen. It was Mom. Sliding my finger across the bottom, her face came into focus.

"Hey, Mark!" she said. "How are you?"

I told her that I was fine, but I was in a time crunch. "I'll be quick, then," she said. "Did you recently spend $800 on your debit card?"

"What?!" I flinched. "I haven't spent anything *close* to that much money down here. I was just about to go to the ATM to make a withdrawal."

"In that case, something's wrong," she said. "I just got a call from the bank telling me that there was a massive overdraft on your account."

An overdraft? How could that be? I've got my wallet and my debit card in my pocket. No one else has touched it.

I was clueless. More than that, I was scared. Money was a rare commodity in Honduras. I relied on what I had in my bank account. Now, even that security had been taken from me.

In that moment, all I knew was that I had no cash and needed to make a trip to the ATM in order to get home. Mom promised to keep in touch with the bank and let me know anything they learned on the matter.

I situated the tablet into my backpack and pulled the two zippers toward each other on both ends. Taking a napkin, I wiped the sweat ring from the table where my mug had been sitting. Then, pulling the straps over my shoulders, I secured my backpack and quickly stepped past the now-vacant tables, through the lobby, out the door, and down the street to the ATM. If I could just get to Oranado without losing myself to panic, I could figure this out later.

I pulled open the glass door leading to the tiny, cramped closet that housed the machine. Glancing over my shoulder, I pulled my wallet from the back pocket of my khaki shorts and found the golden debit card nestled safely inside. I swiped it and carefully typed in the four-digit code to my account. A message appeared on screen:

ERROR:

ACCESO DENEGADO

ACCESS DENIED

I was at a loss. Waiting for the main menu to reappear, I tried again, only to be met with the same message.

Three attempts and three errors later, I gave up. I groaned as I leaned hard against the wall. My hands fell to my side and my eyes wandered back to the glowing screen, now displaying a digital clock.

4:52 p.m.

There was no time to fool around feeling sorry for myself. I could worry about that later. Right now, I had a bus to catch.

My wallet found its way back into my pocket as the glass door closed behind me. My hands clenched tightly to the straps of my backpack as I hurried to the plaza. *What am I going to do now?* I couldn't ask a local for money. In Copán, it was typical to be approached by multiple beggars in one day. Tourists have money—that was the common assumption in those parts. How could I be so audacious as to ask a Honduran for financial help?

David and Shelly would surely come to my rescue. After all, bus fare to Oranado was only ten lempiras—less than fifty cents. I settled on that plan, but quickly realized that I had no method of finding them. Even if I emailed them now and they responded quickly, the bus would be long gone.

I scanned the plaza. In the distance, I noticed two figures sitting atop a large rock eating ice cream. Their pale skin and bohemian attire immediately gave them away as tourists. Surely they had extra money on hand. They were vacationers after all. Besides, how else could they have afforded to buy ice cream?

There was no time to weigh the options. I would either have to swallow my pride and ask, or accept that I was stuck in Copán for the night. I put one foot forward and started for the rock.

The young man and woman sat peacefully, holding their cones while admiring the Catholic Church across the park. They spoke softly to one another between licks. I was close now. How should I start the conversation? In English? Spanish? I stood only a few feet away now. Clearing my throat, I spoke:

"Hi, um, do you guys speak English?" It seemed a bit direct, but there was no time to ease in.

The couple met my face in genuine surprise. They sat in silence for a moment, as if they weren't quite sure what to make of this encounter. Finally, the man said in a British accent, "Yeah, we speak English."

I gave a sigh of relief and continued. "Look, this is really embarrassing. I've never had to do this before." The man gave me a suspicious look. My heart was beating fast. "I teach in a little town about ten minutes from here. There's something wrong with my bank account right now and I'm completely broke." The man could obviously tell where this was going. His face turned from suspicion to impatience. I had to wrap up quick. "I need ten lempiras for a bus ticket home. I know how fishy this seems, but it's only ten lempiras." They stared at me. "Please," I added for good measure.

The girl's expression was hard to read. She seemed indifferent and willing to agree with whatever her partner's decision might be. He looked at her and raised one eyebrow. Then, turning back to me, said, "Uh, no, man. Sorry."

I nodded silently, allowing his answer to sink in. "Well, um, thanks anyway," I said, unsure how to end this awkward confrontation.

I spun around and scanned the plaza once again. There were no other tourists—at least, not obvious ones. If I was going to find anyone that could help, it wouldn't be here. I shot off in the direction of the jewelry tents. Running the length of the road and finding no one, I retraced my steps back to the plaza. One final glance confirmed my fears. There would be no help tonight. I was stuck.

My arms went limp and I slouched against a wall. Enrique had an extra bedroom. I could probably stay with him. But I would be terribly underdressed and completely without my teaching materials at school tomorrow. And who could say how Hissela would react to that? The stress of caring for her sickly mother on top of maintaining a nearly-bankrupt school was obviously taking an emotional toll these days. Oh sure, she still smiled. But beneath her happy exterior was an anxious and worried woman ready to crack. We all knew it, even if no one spoke about it.

Finish strong. Finish strong. Finish...

But how could I even *finish* without money—let alone *finish strong*?

I sighed. *This, God. This is why believing in you is so freakin' hard. Stuff like this happens—stuff you could fix so easily—and you just sit there and do nothing. This is why, if you really do exist, I can't trust you. Because when I do, I'm left out to dry.*

My thoughts were interrupted by a nearby voice, clearly British. "Hey man," the tourist said, approaching me. "Take this." He stretched out his hand, holding a ten between his fingers. I stared with an uncertain expression, but he rattled his hand and said, "Seriously, it's yours." I extended my arm, glancing at the rock where he had been sitting moments ago. His partner gave me a wave and a smile, nodding in reassurance. I took the bill and searched for the right words to thank him.

Coming up with nothing, I simply offered, "Th-thank you. Thank you."

"Good luck to you, mate," he said, turning around and walking back to his rock.

I looked down and examined the money. It was worth less than fifty cents. Yet, so much hung on it. Then I remembered, I had a bus to catch. In an instant I was running down the street to the bus stop. Undoubtedly it was past 5:00, but maybe by some fortune I would get lucky today.

Sure enough, when I arrived, the driver had the hood propped open and was tinkering with the engine. I ran to the door waving the money above my head. The man accepted it and I jumped aboard.

Being the last passenger, I had to stand just in front of the first bench, doubled over with my hand on the driver's seat to keep my balance. The driver hopped inside, turned the engine, and just like that, the bus began its journey down the beaten road. It took a few minutes before my breathing settled back to normal. Only then did I realize how tense my body was. Forcing my muscles to relax, I closed my eyes and assessed the last twenty minutes.

Somebody has either misplaced or stolen every penny in my bank account. I don't have any cash. I just begged for money from a tourist. I'm completely broke. I won't get paid again until God-knows-when...

God. Not ten minutes ago, I'd outright scolded him for leaving me in Copán, followed immediately by a random donation and a seat on a bus to Oranado. I had no choice but to swallow my pride.

Yeah...ok, thanks. I appreciate it. I really do.

I glanced out the window as three dusty figures carrying loaded sacks flew by.

But what about them, God? What about all the poor people here in Honduras?

Twenty faces watched as I held onto the front seat. This was not the time to display my indignation. I tried to focus my attention on other things: Sofía's smile, Aaron's church, cliff jumping at *el salto*, the British couple in Copán. And there I paused. Why *had* the man decided to give me money after blatantly telling me no? What changed his mind?

Sure, it was only ten lempiras, but I might have used it for anything; drugs, alcohol, sex. He had no way of knowing whether I was telling the truth.

I put myself in his shoes. Would I have been willing to help a stranger, especially one who seemed to be the last person in town who needed help? What about in the United States? How many times had I blown off men and women asking for a dollar or two? Some had even asked specifically for bus fare or just enough to call home. It had always been so easy to shoo them away on the grounds of, "they only want booze." Perhaps my British friend assumed as much about me. Still, the only reason I was on a bus to Oranado was on account of his generosity.

Chapter 23

Canadians

My empty wallet kept me in Oranado for nearly a week. Back in Missouri, Mom and Dad worked with the bank to solve the mystery of my overdrafted bank account. A few days into the week, Dad called to let me know that the bank had tracked the spending to Panama; someone had used the ATM in Copán to hack into my account and go on a shopping spree.

Over the next few days, I kept in contact with my parents through video calls and emails. The police were on the case. That was good news, of course, but it didn't help my empty wallet. Mom later informed me that the bank would replace the stolen money and that I should be able to make an ATM withdrawal within the next few hours. The only downside was that I'd have to call my parents, who would then have to call the bank and inform them any time I was about to hit the ATM, giving me a five minute window to take out my cash. It was inconvenient, but it kept my account safe, or so I was told.

After school on Monday, I rode the bus to Copán with the students. I had been in touch with David and Shelly through email over the weekend, and we decided to meet at the British Colonial House that afternoon. It was about the nicest restaurant Copán had to offer. Before meeting my Canadian friends for dinner, I found a Wi-Fi hotspot and called my parents. They, in turn, called the bank, allowing me to pull some money out of the machine. I counted the colorful bills and placed them in my wallet, then walked back to the restaurant. Like everything else in Copán, it was completely open-air. The only glass window was found on the front door, which, of course, was propped wide open.

Being the middle of the afternoon, the three-story restaurant was completely vacant, save for the Canadian couple and a handful of staff. Walking up the first flight of stairs, I poked my head into the dining room and saw David and Shelly sitting at a table near the center of the room. David was scrolling through his tablet, while Shelly studied her Spanish note cards.

"Hey guys," I said, breaking the silence.

They both looked up and offered a wave. "Hey Mark," they said, almost in unison.

"Have a seat," David offered.

"Sorry I'm running a little late," I said, pulling out a chair.

"No problem at all," Shelly said. "We've got the afternoon off. This was our only plan."

"Great," I said.

"Have you been here before?" David asked.

"Once. I made a rule for myself when I first got to Honduras: If I find myself saying 'Someday I'm gonna do this-or-that', I have to do it. There aren't many restaurants left that I haven't tried."

"Wow!" Shelly exclaimed. "That's pretty brave. Do you do that every time you travel?"

I pondered that for a moment. "I guess not. I like to travel, but I don't do it alone very often."

"This must have been a big adjustment for you, then," David said.

I laughed. "Yeah, you could say that."

"So take us through it," Shelly said. "How did you get here? Why Honduras?"

I took a breath and thought for a moment. Just as I began, the waiter arrived and asked what we would like to drink. David and Shelly ordered tea, light ice in David's. I had resolved to drink water that day, but at the last second, I caved in and ordered a Coke instead. This was a special occasion, and as we had all successfully ordered in Spanish, it called for a celebration.

"*Su español suena fantástico. Buen trabajo,* " I said. "I'm really impressed."

"It hasn't been an easy three weeks," David said. "We've spent just about all of our free time studying."

"That's probably what I need to do," I replied. "I might actually learn something."

The waiter looped around the table, dropping off each of our drinks, then made his way back to the kitchen.

"So," Shelly steered the conversation back, "You were saying that you went to school for TESOL."

"Oh yeah." I proceeded to tell my story, condensing it as much as possible. I intentionally left out Taylor's role in the first week, as well as my spiritual crisis. When I got to my three days in Florida, I wrapped it up. "And that's when I met you guys in the airport." David gave a confirming nod. "So, what about you two?" I asked. "Tell me how you ended up here."

The two looked at one another, waiting for the other to begin. "Well," David finally started, still looking at Shelly, "Our Church in Nova Scotia is very involved with a particular ministry in Tegucigalpa." David told me about the ministry that his church had partnered with in Honduras to work with orphans and widows in practical ways. He described their first trip to Honduras, during which they had visited prisons, orphanages, churches, impoverished villages, and shelters for battered women. He and Shelly had fallen in love with the country and were determined to see Jesus bring hope to the hurting.

Up until that point, the subject of God, church, and religion hadn't come up. I wasn't sure where they stood, nor they sure of me. It came as such a relief to hear about their prayers before coming and the ways in which God had lead them to act. I could be honest with these people; there was no need to sugar coat my life.

Near the end of David's story, the waiter came back and asked if we were ready. The Canadians ordered their food in broken Spanish— *chuletas mercado* and *sopa de res*. I ordered *el pollo a la plancha*, as it was among the cheapest menu options. The waiter took down our orders in his small notebook and repeated them back. We nodded in confirmation as he collected our menus and disappeared through the kitchen door.

"That's pretty amazing," I said to David. "All the stuff you're doing with your church. You know, I'm a little disappointed in myself for not telling you that I'm a Christian, too. A lot more has happened in my short time here than I let on earlier."

Shelly set her sweaty glass of tea down on the table and wiped her palm with a handkerchief. "We're all ears," she said.

I clasped my hands beneath the table and looked at Shelly, then to David. "I guess I should start before I even arrived here in Honduras. I was dating this girl named Taylor." I took them through the breakup, explaining that it had been the last straw in my already-lingering doubts about God. I told them that being in Honduras was harder than I could have imagined; I was experiencing loneliness in ways I never had before. I explained the ways in which God had taught me about himself over the past few months. "Being here is so hard," I said. "I keep telling myself to 'finish strong.' But honestly, that's even harder. I'm so tempted to just float by apathetically until June 19. I won't, because, you know, it would be a waste of an amazing opportunity, but it's a feeling I'm constantly fighting."

The waiter had dropped off the food, but no one had taken a bite yet. David said, "That's really tough. We're sorry to hear that's happening." Then he looked at Shelly and said, "Let's pray for the food."

We bowed our heads, because, for whatever reason, that's just what Christians do when they pray. Then David began: "Lord, we're thankful for the food you've provided. Help us to give you glory, even in the little things. And Lord, we're also thankful for the chance to have dinner with Mark and get to know him better. Help him know that you are near, even here in Honduras, and that your Church is everywhere. Even as we do our work in Tegucigalpa, and Mark's Church does your work in the States, and our Church in Canada, help Mark to remember that his work in Oranado is just as important if he does it in your name. And in that name, Jesus, we pray. Amen."

"Amen," Shelly repeated.

We all dug in. I signaled the waiter for another Coke. For a few minutes, no one said anything, except for the occasional comment about how good the food was. "I'm shocked that there are no tortillas," I said. "Literally every meal I've had since coming here has included tortillas." Not a minute later, the waiter arrived at our table with a plate of hot tortillas. "*Buen provecho*," he said, and left us once again.

We looked at each other and broke into laughter. "There it is," I said.

"So, how has it been eating only Hispanic food?" David asked. "Was it quite an adjustment?"

"You guys have been here three weeks," I said. "You've had plenty of time to see exactly what the food is like."

"It's true," Shelly agreed. "The meals all have the same general ingredients: beans, rice, plantains, tortillas."

"You know, it took me like two months before I figured out what plantains were," I said. "I had never eaten them before coming here. Everyone kept calling them *platanos*, and I had no idea what that meant."

"I imagine you've picked up quite a bit of Spanish since then," Shelly said.

"Yeah, I guess." I shrugged, rotating a juicy piece of chicken at the end of my fork. "Everyone told me it would be cake. I honestly thought I would be a pro by now. But there's so much more than just hearing it and picking it up. You have to have an understanding of the mechanics. I kinda wish I could punch everyone in the face that told me I would learn it quickly."

The Canadians laughed. "I can attest to that," David said, raising his glass. He took a sip through the straw and let out a sigh. "I thought learning Spanish would be simple after already having a knowledge of another second language. I'm finding it just as difficult as you are."

We talked for a few minutes about learning Spanish. We agreed that it was probably for the best that we were learning it in the midst of people who spoke it fluently, but that still didn't make it the walk in the park everyone had promised it would be.

The waiter came to take away our empty plates as our conversation lingered. I learned more about their church and I told them about mine. I mentioned that I had been to Canada once, and we discussed the different regions. "Manitoba," David said, "More like Mani*snow*ba." As we reached for our money to set atop the checks, the conversation began to wind down.

Once the bills were settled, it was finished. No one said it. They didn't have to. We knew it was time. "Well, Mark," David said, "We're happy that we got to have dinner with you."

I looked down at the table and let out a soft laugh. "Guys," I said, bringing my head up to meet their eyes, "I've been praying for an opportunity to sit down and unload with someone who understands what this experience is like for months now. I even asked my buddy in Florida to pray that I would meet some Americans that I could have an honest conversation with. I never thought God would send me two Canadians."

"Well, Canada *is* part of America," Shelly said with a smile.

"You've been an answer to a prayer that's been a long time in the making," I told them. "So, thank you."

We rose from our seats and David shook my hand. Shelly went in for a hug. Before we left, I asked the waiter if he would take a picture of the three of us. I handed him my tablet and he snapped two or three.

When I got back to my bedroom in Oranado, I posted the picture on Facebook. Two things came of it:

The first was an email I received later that evening. It was from Shelly. She had seen the picture online and wanted to encourage me. She promised to pray for me every day until June and gave me permission to unload on them any time I needed to.

The second was a comment from a friend in Missouri:

"Oh my god, dude. You are so skinny."

PART FIVE

readjusting

Chapter 24

Guatemala

Semana Santa translates literally as "Holy Week". In Hispanic culture, Semana Santa begins on Palm Sunday and leads up to the following Sunday, Easter. The exact seven-day period changes with the year but the festivities are always the same, and have been for centuries. Every town with a Catholic Church joins in the celebration, decorating the streets with bright colors and holding nightly masses. Enormous crowds of people parade through the streets in reverence, celebration, and awe of Jesus' final week of life (you know, before the whole resurrection thing). There's a freshness, a peacefulness, in the air. Children are given the week off from school. Many businesses close their doors. Families travel the length of entire countries to be together. Everyone is in good cheer with one another.

With Easter being at the end of April, Semana Santa came late that year; I'd been forced to watch as my American friends enjoyed Spring Break a month earlier while I continued teaching. Now the tables had turned. Semana Santa had arrived and before me was an entire week of possibilities.

"What are you going to do for Semana Santa?"

"Hmm?" I set down my pen and looked at Sofía sitting across the cafeteria table. "Sorry, what?"

"Semana Santa," she repeated. "Do you have plans?"

"Not really," I said. "I think I'll just stay at home and watch TV."

She squinted her eyes suspiciously.

"Of course I have plans!" I said. "The second that bell rings this afternoon, I'm taking off my teacher hat and I'm going full-American-tourist. I've got nine days to explore every inch of this place, and that's exactly what I'm gonna do."

"'Explore every inch'? You mean hiking in the mountains?"

"No, I mean Central America. The whole thing."

Sofía was lost.

"I'm going to take a bus to Guatemala," I explained. "Then, when I get back, I'm going to talk to the tourist agency in Copán and see about going to El Salvador for a couple days; hike some volcanoes and stuff. Then, if there's time, I might go check out Honduras a little farther east; maybe stay in Gracias or something."

Sofía's eyes widened. "Are you crazy?!"

"Don't worry," I assured her. "It'll all be super calculated. I'm going to figure out exactly how much money I'll need, and I'll make sure someone knows where I am in case something goes wrong."

"Something *will* go wrong," she shot back. "You are going to get killed, Mark."

I shrugged. "Well, some things are worth dying for. Seeing the world seems to be about the best example I can think of."

"You have no idea what you are doing. This will not end well."

"I'm glad you care so much. But I'm never going to get this opportunity again."

"What if you get lost?" she challenged.

"José says my Spanish is good."

"Oh yes," she said dryly. "And what do *you* think?"

Sofía had me there. She knew I wasn't tremendously confident with my Spanish. I sighed. "I think that traveling down here is cheap, especially internationally. That's something I couldn't say if I was back home. I want this, Sofía. I *need* this adventure."

"Ok, Mark," Sofía said, throwing her hands into the air and rolling her eyes. "Have fun on your adventure. I hope you are still alive in a week." She closed her notebook and collected her supplies, then got up and walked through the cafeteria.

"Sofía," I called, stopping her in her tracks. "If something did happen... Would you miss me?"

She turned around and nodded silently. "I know you. You do stupid things without thinking first. Please, just be careful."

"Ok," I promised.

For a moment, nothing was said. We looked at one another, watching as the breeze lightly ruffled the other's hair and clothes. At last,

I broke the silence.

"Seriously, though, If I do die this week, my classes' book reports are due on May 21."

Sofía rolled her eyes and turned around before a smile could betray her scowl. "*Gringos estúpidos*," she said, just loud enough so I could hear it.

"I'd miss you, too," I whispered as she disappeared around the corner.

I spent Saturday in Copán as usual. Sunday was fairly standard as well, with the exception of the Catholic procession in the street, which I quickly ran outside to join. When Monday arrived, I dumped the books and papers from my backpack, stuffing t-shirts and clean boxer shorts into the pockets where I found room. Pulling the bedside drawer open, I found my passport and placed it securely in the front pocket, then zipped it tight. It was all too familiar.

The day was young and the sun floated high in the cloudless sky. The bus driver took the folded twenty from my hand, replacing it with a ten, and just like that, we were on our way to Copán. Upon arriving, I hustled to the nearest Wi-Fi hot spot and called home. Mom got ahold of the bank back in Missouri and informed them that I was about to withdraw some money in Honduras. My five-minute window was open. I rushed to the enclosed ATM on the side of the road. I swiped my card, typed in my pin, and selected English. Fifteen hundred lempiras should be enough for a two-day trip to Guatemala. Collecting my money, I left the enclosure and retraced my steps to call Mom back.

"I'm all done at the ATM," I told her. "Thanks."

She was glad to help. Little did she know that I was headed to another country in a matter of minutes. All the better. There was no need to worry my parents. I'd barely made it to that point after Sofía's lecture. How much more would Mom and Dad fret over my safety? I was tired of insisting to everyone that I'd be fine. No one needed to know my plans for Semana Santa, so that's who I told. Besides, I'd only planned to be in Guatemala for one day. What could possibly go wrong?

The ride to the border brought with it another wave of

memories—none of them fond. I had taken this bus before, seen the trees and road just beyond the invisible border, and been turned away. *Not this time*, I thought. *This time I'm the king, and Chiquimula is my throne.*

The bus moved up and down the winding road. For the second time, I saw Marlon's house zip by on the right. At this point, a young boy held out his hand toward the passengers. People began digging in their pockets for bus fare. I reached over the seat and handed him a twenty and a ten. "*Cuarenta*," he said, passing the bills back to me.

Forty lempiras? Did it cost that much last time? I shrugged it off, remembering José's words: "Without sacrifice, there is no victory." I added a ten to the stack and passed it forward.

The bus arrived at the border in exactly the same way it had before. The side doors opened and we filed out, one by one. This time, though, I was the only gringo among the passengers. As soon as my feet hit the dirt, I headed straight for the Honduran Customs building, and pulled open the glass door. I held my breath, hoping, *praying*, not to see the border guard from last time.

I poked my head inside. The room was empty, but for the small line leading to the desk. An unfamiliar man sat behind it, inspecting passports and counting money. *Perfect.*

The line moved fairly quickly. When my turn came, I handed my passport over and watched as the guard opened it directly to the back page and added a stamp. I was charged one hundred lempiras for entry into Guatemala.

"*Gracias*," I thanked the man, then turned to leave. The door closed behind me as I turned left, stepping foot into neutral territory. Honduras was now behind me, Guatemala ahead.

Adrenaline shot through my entire body, sending chills down both arms. The unbridled ecstasy of crossing a border into a country I'd never been in overtook me. My walk soon became a sprint. *I'm so happy right now, I could die.* I stopped just shy of the *Bienvenidos a Guatemala* sign, then, taking a deep breath, heaved myself over the border with a giant leap.

Two men holding leather bags stared at me with confused expressions. They watched as I continued skipping deeper into the country, then called out, "*Amigo!*" I turned around to see them coming toward me. *"Necesitas cambiar tu dinero?"* the first man asked, holding up his satchel and pulling a handful of foreign currency from it.

Of course! You have to exchange your Honduran money for Guatemalan, you dummy. This just keeps getting better and better.

I handed the man every last lempira in my wallet, as he pecked a few keys on his small calculator. He held the screen up so that I could see the number. I nodded to confirm this was accurate, having no idea what the exchange rate was. He presented me with a stack of slick, colorful bills, starkly different from the currency I'd come to know so well since January.

"Cómo se llaman?" I asked. *What are these called?*

"Quetzals," the man said.

"Quetzals," I repeated. "Cool. *Gracias."*

The men bid me farewell as I continued my trek into the new land. Truth be told, there was absolutely no aesthetic difference between the two countries. Had there been no measures to keep illegal immigration at bay, it would have been impossible to tell where one country ended and another began. Still, just knowing I was walking on foreign soil put a skip in my step. Literally.

Up ahead, a myriad of busses were parked along the road. I followed behind a little old lady carrying a plastic bag full of fabric as she made her way toward the only bus with an open door. She slowly pulled herself up and took a seat inside.

A man leaned against the driver-side door, puffing on a cigarette. "Chiquimula?" I asked before hopping board. He gave a single nod and stared ahead through his dark sunglasses, as if I was nothing more than a voice in his head.

Only a handful of people had boarded the fifteen passenger van-bus. I took a row for myself and rested my legs on the seat. A few minutes later, the shuttle was off, ferrying its small band of travelers deeper into the west.

Passing through a small cluster of homes, the bus stopped to pick up a man waving just off the road. Behind him, a family stood outside a yellow shack, watching the road. The men were dressed relatively similar to those in Honduras—blue jeans, cowboy hats, dusty t-shirts—but here the women all wore bright, colorful, frilly dresses. Perhaps it was on account of Semana Santa; I'd seen nothing like it in Honduras.

As we ventured deeper into Guatemala, the forest began to thin out. Mountains turned rockier and browner, until the lush quasi-jungles of the east yielded completely to the barren, dry desert that consumed the land.

Two hours passed, and still we drove. At one point, the bus inched slowly through a mid-size city full of cars, buildings, and paved streets. A couple passengers called to the driver. The bus slowed down—never completely stopping—as the couple opened the side door, jumped out, and slammed it shut behind them. "*Es esta Chiquimula?*" I asked the driver. He shook his head silently and drove steadily onward. As we left civilization behind, the fear of missing my destination slowly began creeping deep into my mind. What if I missed Chiquimula and wound up in the wild Guatemalan west? How far from Copán would I go before conceding that skipping town without telling anyone might not have been the brightest idea? *Not far enough. Not yet.*

Farther and farther we drove, until at last, the bumpy road began to smooth out. Before long, we were moving with the steady flow of highway traffic. The bus swerved to the right, barely making it onto a ramp, then slammed on the brakes to avoid missing a merging truck on the left. We continued along the road for another mile before the scenery changed completely.

A thriving metropolis had sprouted up from the desert. Giant buildings towered above the traffic in every direction. Unlike the buildings in Honduras—even San Pedro Sula and Santa Rosa—these buildings were covered in dark, shiny glass. There was almost no barbed wire or barred windows in sight. Multiple lanes of painted and paved roads multiplied and split at every corner, bringing the throng of mopeds and vans to a halt as stop lights changed from green to red. This city was far bigger and livelier than any I had set foot in since December. The hustle and bustle of the vehicle and foot traffic was enough to convince anyone they were in Manhattan.

The bus slowed to a crawl as it pulled into the right lane, and the driver announced, "*Chiquimula!*" The man in front of me pulled open the side door and hopped out. I followed suit, catching my balance as my feet hit the pavement. And just like that, the driver sped away and the bus was gone. A horn honked loudly behind me. Without a second thought, I leapt onto the sidewalk, giving the car room to pass.

I am definitely not in Oranado anymore.

Hotel first. Then food.

That was the only plan I had.

I followed the sidewalk as traffic flew by on my left. There was never a moment of silence in this place. Even in the brief seconds when the street emptied out, holding the next wave of vehicles hostage at the traffic light, the sounds of engines, car horns, chatter, and industrial racket blared from the nearby blocks and bounced from building to building, filling the stretch of road with the song of the city.

There was no indication of a hotel district, no signs to point pedestrians in any certain direction. I walked aimlessly, turning this way and that down unfamiliar roads. I had completely lost all sense of where I was in relation to where the bus had dropped me off. And I loved every second of it.

Fifteen minutes passed, then thirty, then an hour. I pressed onward through the bustling city until I came to the first sign I recognized: Domino's Pizza. The neon red letters shone brightly over a large plaza. In the center stood a tall fountain. The perimeter was lined with shops and restaurants. A gargantuan Catholic church watched over the plaza, as pedestrians mingled and traffic raced by. This must have been the center of town.

Being my only familiar landmark, I walked toward the pizza shop. Behind the restaurant stood a tall, concrete building with a white, wooden sign hanging above the front door: *Hotel*.

Just inside the hotel door sat a fragile old lady behind a desk. Her silver hair fluttered in the breeze of an oscillating fan. "*Cómo estás hoy?*" she asked, turning to me. I told her I needed a room for the night and asked how much. "*Noventa quetzals*," she replied. I counted out ninety and handed the money over the desk. She scribbled down some notes and reached into a drawer, pulling out a key. Attached was a wooden keychain, displaying a handwritten "45" on the front. She placed it on the counter and told me to make sure I was out by 11:00 tomorrow morning.

I found room 45 on the second floor. The numbers were nailed halfway down the door, barely covering some minor graffiti. I inserted the key and turned the knob, taking a good look at the room before me. It was nothing fancy: one twin-sized bed, a dresser attached to a small wooden desk, a box TV mounted on the wall, and a shoddy bathroom. The concrete floor was uncarpeted, and echoed as I dropped my bag.

In that moment, more than ever before in my life, I felt like an adult. Even at twenty-five, it was hard not to feel eighteen most days. I had been in college most of those years and was nowhere *near* being married. Heck, I worked in fast food back in Missouri. Now I stood in a hotel room that I had located and paid for all by myself in a city I had traveled to alone on my nine-day break from classroom teaching in a foreign country. A deep sense of pride and accomplishment swelled in me as I plopped onto the bed and made myself comfortable in my new home-away-from-home-away-from-home.

Transportation was different in Chiquimula. Rather than boarding a bus and waiting for it to reach full capacity, Chiquimula employed multiple busses to drive the streets in a set course. The side doors were removed, allowing pedestrians to jump aboard at any point and pay a flat rate of two quetzals.

Obviously that meant I had to give it a try. The driver slowed his shuttle when he saw me waving my hand, and waited for me to board. We picked up speed and were soon deep among the steady flow of traffic. The driver weaved in and out of city blocks, finally merging onto the highway. Keeping in the right lane, we took the first exit ramp and came to a large building surrounded by a full parking lot. The walls were lined with business signs. I recognized it immediately: a shopping mall.

Dropping two coins into the driver's styrofoam cup between the front seats, I hopped out and found the automatic double doors leading inside. Straight ahead, two vending machines stood in the center of the hallway, parting foot traffic to opposite sides and illuminating their backs in its radiance.

José had told me about the Coca-Cola in Guatemala, that even as delicious as Coke was in Honduras, it didn't hold a candle to Guatemalan Coke. It was time to put that claim to the test. Pulling some change from my pocket, then slipping it into the slot, I waited for the thud and pulled my prize from behind the flap. It fizzed and crackled as I untwisted the lid and brought the plastic bottle to my mouth. One taste was all it took. My eyes nearly bulged out of their sockets as the sweet, heavenly liquid flowed from my tongue to my stomach. The game had changed completely.

The hallway opened up to reveal two stories of shops, none of which I recognized. Still, simply standing in a shopping mall was rejuvenating. Like so many other things, I hadn't realized how much I missed such a simple experience until I was face to face with it. Even with all the Spanish, it felt just like home.

I walked around for an hour or two, taking it all in and exploring the food court options. *Comida China it is*.

Chiquimula must not have attracted many visitors. Puzzled faces watched as the lone gringo carried his food to the vacant table in the corner. It didn't matter. I was going to enjoy every millisecond of this short vacation in a lost paradise.

After dinner, I made a trip downstairs to visit the two-screen movie theater. Two posters hung behind the glass display case: *Rio 2* and *Noah*. I glanced at the showtimes. If I bought a ticket right now, I could be sitting in the theater watching *Rio 2* in fifteen minutes. I'd never seen the first *Rio*. It didn't matter.

"*Uno para Rio 2*," I told the man in the ticket booth.

There was nothing spectacular about the theater, except it was just that. I hadn't been to a theater in five months. This experience felt far more American than anything I had done in Florida. With my euphoria came a shocking surprise: I understood the entire movie, even in Spanish! In my unrestrained joy, I found a particular scene much funnier than the audience around me. I laughed louder and harder than anyone else in the packed theater, far longer than the joke had meant to be laughed at. Heads darted from side to side to find the obnoxious laughter, but when they realized it was coming from the silly gringo in the front row, they started laughing as well. Before long, the entire theater was overcome with unbridled laughter. Normally I would have felt dumb. That night, I welcomed it.

After the movie, I caught a shuttle back into the city. The driver was eager to be rid of me and asked if he could drop me off a few blocks early. I told him it was fine and hopped out through the doorway. It took a bit longer than anticipated, but I finally came within sight of the blinding neon Domino's sign. Once in my hotel room, I removed my shirt and fell onto the hard mattress. I snatched the remote and turned on the television. News, news, soap opera, porn, news, infomercial, porn. *Click*. The room went black again.

I put my arms behind my head and stared at the ceiling. The noisy city penetrated the cement walls and filled the room with its muffled voice. *Today was perfect*. The more I thought about it, the more I despised the idea of spending a fortune to sleep in a fancy hotel room. This room, even in its simplicity, was more than enough for an adventure like this. All I needed was a bed and a bathroom. Vacations should be spent exploring and having fun, not cooped up inside a bedroom with all the accommodations of home. I decided then and there that if I ever traveled the world, I would spend the majority of my money on transportation and the rest on getting lost in the culture. Hotels make far too much money on providing the luxuries of home and sucking away the adventure that is begging to be had.

"Good night, Guatemala," I said aloud. "Happy Semana Santa."

Chapter 25

Between the Border

I awoke to the familiar sound of my digital alarm. It was 9:00. I would have been perfectly content to stay in bed long past noon, but I was on a time constraint. Unless I wanted to risk my dwindling budget and fork over another ninety quetzals, I needed to be up and out by 11:00.

I took my first (and only) hot shower in Central America. It was a welcome relief, having spent nine hours next to the roaring window unit shoveling cold air into the tiny cement bedroom. As I packed up my belongings, I tried the television again. To my surprise and joy, I stumbled across an episode of Veggie Tales. The picture was snowy and the characters spoke in cartoony Spanish, but I was happy to compromise.

Eventually, I killed the power to the screen, turned off the air, and locked the door, leaving the room behind as I descended the stairs. Returning the key to the front desk, I walked to the plaza for a new day of Guatemalan exploration. I discovered a few fountains and statues scattered throughout the city. Bright flowers accented the doors and windows of shops in honor of Semana Santa. Colored sawdust had been poured onto the ground in beautiful patterns and shapes, all in preparation of the upcoming Catholic processions.

When I finally gave in to my hunger, I hopped on a shuttle and stayed aboard until it arrived at the mall. I knew exactly where I was headed today. The golden arches had called out to me the night before. That morning, their cry was even louder.

I'd never been so thankful to be a Gentile as I unfolded the thin tissue paper and bit into my Sausage Mcgriddle. At that moment, McDonald's was the most wonderful company in the world. Two Sausage Mcgriddles and three hash browns later, I waddled into the shopping mall and made another quick round of window-shopping. It would have to get me through until June 19. I glanced at the show times as I passed the movie theater. *Noah* would start in ten minutes, and the mall was relatively empty. I decided to give it a go.

Food was the last thing on my mind. But when I passed the concession stand and saw the popcorn, I couldn't resist. I gave into my American cravings and bought one large bag and a Coke. To my surprise, the theater was completely empty; I had the entire movie to myself. I tossed my feet onto the seat before me and unloaded my concessions onto the vacant seat to my right. The dim lights grew pitch-black and the movie began. As if things weren't perfect already, the movie was completely in English. Spanish subtitles ran along the bottom of the screen, but not a word was spoken. "Sweet!" I shouted, shoving a handful of buttery popcorn into my mouth and sipping down the best Coke I'd ever tasted.

For the next two hours, I was in my own private America.

I could not have found the bus stop from the previous day if my life depended on it. It was only by chance that I stumbled onto a bustling street filled with busses loading and unloading. A man stood holding the roof of a particular bus with one foot hanging from the door as it inched alongside the road. He looked at me and put his hand out.

"*A la frontera?*" I called over the purr of a hundred idling engines. *To the border?*

"*Sí!*" came his reply.

Running to catch up, I threw my backpack through the open door and climbed aboard. With that, the man smacked the roof twice and closed the door as the driver put the pedal to the metal.

This driver clearly had no regard for anyone on the road but himself. More than once, the bus came within inches of smashing headfirst into oncoming traffic. Pedestrians weren't safe, wildlife wasn't safe, and we, the passengers, certainly weren't safe. We barreled down a steep incline just outside of town and everyone on board was sent flying into the seatback in front of them. The driver wasn't phased at all. As long as the bus arrived at the border, he was getting paid.

When we did arrive at the border, I opened my wallet to count what money I had left from the trip. I was pushing it, but I decided I should have just enough to get across the border and back to Oranado. Walking first to Guatemalan Customs, I paid the guard and made my way across the invisible line into no man's land. Before I could even open the door to Honduran Customs, the moneychangers were pulling me aside. I handed the man everything in my wallet, keeping one quetzal for myself. *I have to bring something back from Guatemala.*

He counted the stack, crunched some numbers, presented me with his calculator to confirm the transaction, and passed back a small handful of lempiras. *It's nice to have normal money again*, I thought. Then, realizing the absurdity of the thought, I laughed and secured the money safely in my wallet.

Pulling the glass door open and walking into the wide, open lobby, I was pleased to find no line. But that wasn't my only surprise. Just behind the desk sat a lady in a pitch black uniform—the very same guard who had denied me permission into Guatemala two months earlier.

This was different, though. I had nothing to worry about now. I'd made it into Guatemala with no problems. Surely I was legal and safe. Still, the memory of our last encounter caused my heart to beat twice as fast. I swallowed hard and walked to the desk, pulling my passport from my pocket. I slid it over the desk and took out my wallet to pay the small entry fee. She looked it over and flipped a few pages. Her eyes moved from the small blue document to my face. Did she recognize me? Her poker face was flawless.

Finally, she slid the passport back over the desk, and calmly informed me that I couldn't enter Honduras. I cocked my head and lowered my eyebrows, staring silently as I processed the words in my head.

"Um...*por qué?*" I finally managed.

Her Spanish was fast and fluid. She clearly wasn't interested in taking the time of day to help an ignorant gringo understand Central American immigration laws. From what I could make out, she said that I had been in Honduras longer than ninety days and I was legally obligated to leave this part of Central America before I could cross any more international borders. I told her that there must be a misunderstanding; I'd crossed the border yesterday without problems. It must have been a careless mistake, she said.

I explained that I'd gone to the United States only a few weeks prior for this very reason. There was no documentation, I was told. She took back the passport and flipped through the pages, proving her accusation. I snatched it and examined the pages for myself. Sure enough, the United States hadn't stamped my passport upon reentry in Tampa.

I tried desperately to explain where I had stayed in Florida two months ago. She asked if I had any proof—a plane ticket, perhaps? I thought for a moment, remembering that I had thrown away my ticket in San Pedro Sula shortly before meeting David and Shelly at the airport. I shook my head at the guard. "No," I said, lowering my head.

A thought suddenly occurred to me. If I could access my email, I could show her my flight confirmation and itinerary. Searching for the right words, I slowly and painfully explained my plan as she rolled her eyes and asked me to move out of the line, as two men had stepped up.

Pulling my tablet from my backpack, I opened the settings and held it out in hopes of connecting to Wi-Fi. A weak signal was detected, but required a password. I left the building in desperate hope that I might stumble upon a gust of internet coming from one of the nearby shops. After ten minutes of walking in circles outside the Customs office, I gave up. Two more shacks were visible just across the border. Perhaps if I could just get close enough, I could connect.

I entered the building and waved to the guard, calling her attention. I announced that I was going back into Guatemala for a few minutes. "*No.*" I wouldn't be crossing any more borders until this situation was resolved. I was legally trapped between two countries.

I was nowhere, and getting back to "somewhere" was completely out of the question.

I asked what my options were. She said I would either need to provide proof of my international departure before my first ninety days, or else I'd be forced to get on a bus that would take me to Belize and return after three days. The trip was two full days each way. Not only would I arrive back in Oranado *after* school started next week, but literally no one on Earth would know my whereabouts.

The trip would require multiple bus connections and fees. I

certainly couldn't afford the trip, and even if I could, my banking situation wouldn't allow me access to an ATM. Spending three days homeless in Belize only added to the danger I faced as an American.

My head was spinning a million miles an hour. All I could think of was Sofía's face as she stared at me from across the cafeteria table. "You have no idea what you are doing, Mark. This will not end well."

"Uh-hum," the guard cleared her throat emphatically, seizing my full attention. I blinked rapidly, unable to say another word. She informed me that she was preparing to put her plan into effect if I couldn't come up with anything soon—*very* soon. I begged for a little more time and left the building again. I was at a stalemate. Her plan was unthinkable. This was no longer an adventure; it was a risk that would cost far more than I could pay—perhaps my very life.

I gave a hopeless moan and sat down on the curb.

I'm in too deep. This is it.

God...

Ugh, what's the point? I had this coming. And this time there's no one around to bail me out. So much for finishing strong.

My arms rested on my bent knees and my gaze drifted to the ground. That's when a pair of legs walked by and stopped just short of me.

"*Estas bien, amigo?*" a voice asked from above.

I kept my gaze on the street and shrugged.

"*Tal vez puedo ayudarte,*" he said, offering his help.

I looked up to see the face from whence the voice had spoken. A young man towered above me, wearing a bright green polo. On his left breast was stitched a circular patch labeled "*Turismo Honduras.*"

Turismo? Tur...tur...tourism? Honduran Tourism?

It was worth a shot.

I told the man that I was trying to get into Honduras, but wasn't allowed to leave this small patch of land between the two countries. He promptly called out to two others, a man and a woman, wearing matching polos and quickly relayed my situation to them. He then turned my direction asked me to tell them the entire story.

I stood to my feet and took them in with my eyes. Explaining my story in enough detail to make a case for myself would be difficult—

almost impossible in Spanish. What else could I do? I was completely out of options. Closing my eyes and drawing a breath, I began.

I told them *everything* I could think of, incorporating every insignificant, miniscule detail. I spoke for longer than I ever had in Spanish, recalling words that had been mentioned only once or twice by José in Spanish class. At a certain point, I stopped premeditating my sentences altogether and simply allowed them to flow as they came to mind. The Hondurans nodded and squinted to affirm that they were keeping up as I stumbled over words and quickly corrected myself. Once I was sure that I had covered every minor detail and realized that there was nothing more to say, I stopped. It was so abrupt that it took them a moment before realizing that I was finished.

I was absolutely exhausted.

The trio looked at one another and murmured a few sentences back and forth. One man informed me that he was going into Customs to speak with the guard. The other pulled an Android phone from his pocket and opened the internet browser. He placed it in my hand and instructed me to find the flight information in my email. The woman retrieved a flip phone from her purse and began making phone calls. She spoke into her cell phone in a very professional manner, shooting a glance my way every few seconds.

Soon, the trio reconvened, speaking quickly to one another and then looking at me. The first man first asked how long I'd been studying Spanish. Just a few months, I told him. He looked to his partners, eyes open wide, and told me that he was impressed. He then asked if I had found the email. I told him I had. They led me back inside and straight to the desk. The first man leaned in and spoke with the guard, who barely paid notice to me as I stood directly before her. She took the phone and examined the screen closely.

At last, she handed the phone back to the man. Pulling a small sheet of paper from the desk, she jotted some notes and then turned her attention to me. This time, she spoke slowly and loudly, enunciating each syllable. Looking directly into my eyes, she informed me that I would be allowed to enter Honduras, but it would be of the utmost importance that I come back to the office tomorrow morning at 8:00 with as much proof of my story as possible. I needed to bring flight information, teaching forms, immigration slips—anything that would provide evidence of my legal right to be in the country. If I didn't show up, I would be in danger of arrest. "*Me entiendes?*" she asked, making sure I understood.

Every eye in the room was glued to me. Even those who had, until now, been working on other tasks stared in stone cold silence

"*Sí,*" I answered with a single nod.

For a moment, she held my gaze. Her stare almost dared me to try something. Of course, that was the last thing on my mind. She was the alpha, and she wanted to make absolutely sure that I understood that. When she finally blinked, her eyes dropped down to the papers laid out on the desk. She went right back to work, as if to let me know that I was of no more concern to her. I turned around and met eyes with my rescuers. They nodded, confirming that the worst had passed.

But it hadn't.

Chapter 26

Facing Facts

Asking Hissela for help was the last thing I wanted to do. She was at her wits end, and I'd long since passed my limit of mistakes. Ever since Florida, things had been tense. She never mentioned it outright, but I always got the feeling that I was just another hassle on her plate. Try as I might to convince myself otherwise, I knew something was off.

I arrived in Oranado late in the afternoon, and spent the following few hours in my bedroom. How would I tell her that I had crossed the international border alone? What would she think? What would she *say*? When I finally mustered the courage to leave my room, I found her sitting in the kitchen alone. She held lightly to a coffee mug resting on the table. I could barely make out the steam from the mug in the dim light.

"Sorry to bother you," I said, climbing the top few stairs.

"Oh, come in," she replied.

Hissela wore a smile every moment of every day—even when she was unhappy. It was almost impossible to guess what in the world she was thinking. Could she have had any idea what was coming?

"I hate to ask," I began, taking a seat across the table, "but I need some help."

"Oh yes?" she asked, holding her expression.

I sighed. There was no time to dance around it. "Yesterday, I took a bus to Guatemala." I paused, waiting for a reaction. Nothing. "Well, I stayed there overnight and tried to come back today—like, a few hours ago. And they wouldn't let me across the border, because my passport wasn't up to date." Still nothing. "So, um...I made it here, but the border guard said if I don't go back tomorrow morning with proof of my legal right to be in the country, they'll arrest me. And I...I don't know what I should do, and um, I was hoping...I was hoping you could help."

Hissela removed her glasses and set them on the table. She blinked a few times, then took a sip of coffee. "You went to Guatemala alone," she clarified.

I nodded.

"Did you tell anyone you were going?" she asked.

"Well, I, uh, I told Sofía."

"Sofía," she repeated.

"Well," I stammered. "I mean, I...I told her that I *wanted* to go."

Hissela kept her stare. My hands were fidgeting madly beneath the tabletop. I nearly considered praying for invisibility.

Finally, she spoke. "What the hell is wrong with you?" And for the first time since January, her smile faded.

"I'm..."

"No. *What. the hell.* is wrong with you? You think because you are American that you are Superman? Why can you not understand? I have told you that Americans *die* here all the time. Is that what you want? You want to be dead?"

"I just didn't think..."

"Yes! That is the problem! You do not think! You go walking through the mountains alone without telling anyone where you are going, following men with machetes..."

"How did you know about..."

"Your students are twelve years old, Mark. You think they do not talk about the stories you tell them in class?"

I slumped in my chair.

"The children look up to you," she said. "You cannot be so foolish to think that there will be no consequences for your actions."

"I'm sorry," I whispered, partly to myself.

"I am trying to run a school," she pressed on. "Most children in this country do not finish sixth grade. I want to make a difference. I want to see a generation of Honduran children go to college and change this country for their children and their children's children. Can you understand why this is so important?"

I nodded silently.

"But so much of my energy is spent on *you*," she said, pointing. "I see you sneak out of the house after dark and I wonder if you will come back. I wake up one morning and find a letter in the kitchen telling me that you are going to Florida for a week. I have a cup of coffee on the *second day* of Semana Santa and you come to tell me that you are going to be arrested. And why? Because you went to another country by yourself without telling anyone! What am I to do, Mark?"

We sat in silence, both staring at the table. Every few seconds, she opened her mouth, as if she was going to say something, but closed it instead and shook her head with a deep sigh.

"The students love you," she said at last. "What would I tell them if something happened to you? What would I tell your family in the United States?"

Silence overtook the room again. Every second was an eternity. Finally, she stood to her feet and slid the chair beneath the table. "Find all the proof of your trip to Florida that you can," she said. "Set it here on the table tonight with your passport. I will fix this in the morning." With that, she left the room.

I needed to print my flight itinerary. It was the only bit of proof I had to offer, and I knew of only one person who could help. Slipping on a pair of tennis shoes, I left the house and sprinted down the dark road until José's home was within sight.

"What's up, man?" he said, standing in the door.

"I'm in trouble." I frantically recapped the last two days as José listened intently. "I need a printer. You don't happen to have one, do you?"

"No," he said. "I do not. But I know someone who does. We can walk. He only lives a few minutes away."

We set off at once, walking quickly and quietly. Whether my breathing or pace gave it away, José quickly realized that I was exhausted. "Hey man," he said, "let's just take it easy for a minute, ok?"

I leaned against a tree and wiped the sweat from my stubbled head, then covered my eyes with one hand.

After a moment, José asked, "Are you alright, man?"

I shook my head. "No."

He put on arm against the tree and rested his weight. "What is going on?"

My hand fell to my side and our eyes met. I sighed. "José, I'm so tired of being in Honduras. I know it's your home and all; I'm sorry. It's just that...it's just that every time things start to level out, something goes wrong and suddenly I've got a warrant out for my arrest, or Hissela is pissed off at me, or I get dumped, or my bank account gets hacked." I slid the length of the tree until my butt hit the ground. "I'm trying so hard. I just freakin' miss home."

José nodded and took a seat next to me. "You have only a few weeks left, man."

"It's too long."

"Listen, man, soon you will be back in the U.S. You should not be upset that life is not easy. You are only here for a little while. I have lived my entire life in Honduras."

"Yeah, but you're used to it."

"Of course I am. But this does not mean that I like it. You travel for fun. You have opportunities for good jobs. You own a car. Man, these things are not easy for us here. The people of Honduras are jealous of you, Mark."

At that, I fell silent. José's statement was so profound, so humbling. In that moment, I felt stripped of any and all dignity. I was naked and ashamed. How could I have said something so audacious to someone who had so little, who was preparing to leave everything behind for the sake of his wife and daughter?

"You're right, José," I said in a low voice. "I'm sorry."

He waved it off, moving past it just as quickly as it had come up. Standing to his feet, he extended his hand and helped me up. "Ready?" he said.

I nodded. "Yeah." And with that, we were on our way once again.

"Hey," I broke the silence after a few paces. José turned to look at me. "Thanks again for all the help."

"It is no problem," he said.

"I don't just mean tonight," I said. "You've been like a brother to me down here. So just, thanks."

José rested a hand on my shoulder. "You are a good guy, Mark," he said. "You just worry too much."

"I know..."

"What do I always tell you, man? You *cannot* worry."

"I know, but..." I tried again, but José cut me off.

"What did Jesus say about worrying? You cannot add a single minute to your life by worrying. If God takes care of the birds, he is going to take care of you, man. *Do not worry.*"

I left the printed flight itinerary on the kitchen table that night and went to bed. I was up and ready to go by 6:00 the next morning, but Hissela told me that it would be better if I stayed at the house. She and her secretary would make the trip to the border and plead my case alone. I couldn't be sure whether she thought I would say something stupid or she simply didn't want me in her sight. I imagine it was a bit of both.

Things were different after that morning—awkward, forced. We didn't talk much anymore. She still smiled when we passed one another in the hall, and I still turned in my class reports on time. Business went on as usual; no one ever talked about Semana Santa. But a heavy tension now lingered over the roof, both at home and school.

The legalities were settled that morning. I needn't worry about being arrested, but I didn't dare press my luck again. It would be two days before I even got the courage to go to Copán again. I didn't travel farther than that for the rest of Semana Santa.

Chapter 27
Fútbol & Fine Cigars

"Your Semana Santa sounds terrible."

Sofía and I sat side by side in the cafeteria watching as the morning fog hovered between the mountains just across the path.

"It sucked for a little bit," I answered. "But by the weekend things were ok. Guatemala was awesome," I added. "It was a completely different culture, but, like, at times it felt like I was back home."

"I am just glad that you are alive," she said. "I was so worried about you last week."

I laughed. "Apparently you weren't the only one."

"I told you," she said with a hint of pride.

"Hey, I appreciate it. I've only got a few weeks left to not get myself killed. There are still one or two more things on the list."

"You have a *list*?" she asked with genuine surprise.

"Well..." I thought for a moment. "No, I guess not. I've just got a few things I want to do before I go back home."

"Oh. What kinds of things?"

"Um, let me think," I said, looking to the mountains. "Well, I definitely need to watch a soccer game in a bar."

"Why?" Sofía looked at me confused.

"Because back home nobody cares about soccer. Down here it's more important than breathing. I just want to experience one soccer game in my life that I can get excited about."

Sofía wasn't convinced, but offered a smile at the absurdity of it. "Ok, what else?"

I ran a hand over the stubble on my head. "Um, I'd kinda like to smoke a cigar while I'm here."

She winced. "I did not know that you smoke."

"I don't. I've never smoked anything in my life. But I'm in

Central America. You guys grow tobacco by the ton down here. I feel like I owe it to myself to smoke at least one homegrown cigar."

Sofía shrugged in apathetic agreement. "Ok, go to a soccer game and smoke a cigar. Anything else?"

"Well," I started, "I was hoping to find a pretty lady and take her to get coffee." I met Sofía's eyes as another smile crept across her face.

"Why would you do that?" she asked.

I let out a laugh, realizing I'd have to explain myself. "Well, in the U.S., guys and girls...they go to coffee shops when they want to, like...you know...get to know each other. Something about drinking coffee makes it easier to talk, I guess."

"I do not think that is true," she said with a grin. "I think you are the only person who thinks that."

"You don't believe me?"

"Mark, coffee is not romantic. It is just...coffee."

"Yeah, well maybe to someone who drinks fifty gallons a day. Coffee back home is expensive and people don't usually start drinking it until college."

"Oh, *pobrecito*. It must be hard to pay for something that babies drink for free in Honduras." She waited to make sure the jab had set in. "At least when you take a girl to drink coffee in the U.S., she knows that you like her enough to pay."

"If our coffee was half as good as it is here, I could buy a girl one cup and ask her to marry me," I said.

Sofía laughed again. "You are ridiculous."

A few days had passed when Sofía pulled me aside during lunch.

"There is a soccer game at 1:30 on Friday," she told me. "My friend invited me to go to *La Cantina de Don Julio* to watch it with her."

"How are you planning to make it there in time?" I asked. "School won't be over by then."

"We have a half-day this Friday," she reminded me. "Do you want to come with me? You could cross it off of your pretend list."

"Are you sure your friend doesn't want this to be a girls-only-thing?" I asked.

"She will not mind if I bring a cute boy."

"Fiiiiine," I answered, drawing out the word as long as possible. "I guess I'll go, but only because you're forcing me."

"Good," she said, "because I already told her you would be there."

With that, she turned around, nearly smacking me in the face with her ponytail, and walked back to the cafeteria. Only then did I notice the small group of girls peeking out from behind the shed. They giggled and then scattered in all directions.

That Friday, I rode the bus to Copán after school. The students were surprised when I climbed inside and took a seat beside Sofía.

"Mee-stair, why are you coming to Copán today?" Gabriel asked.

"I have a hot date," I told them, shifting my eyebrows up and down.

The girls gasped through their wide smiles and whispered to one another gleefully, while a few boys patted my shoulder with conniving grunts. Sofía smiled bashfully and stared forward without a word. Enrique simply nodded and said, "Yes, well, it is about time."

Once we arrived in Copán, Sofía lifted her little daughter from the bus and set her down gently on the dirt. She immediately wandered to the end of the bus and disappeared from sight. "Victoria!" Sofía called, watching as she reappeared with an outstretched hand. Sofía took hold of her tiny hand and we started off toward *La Cantina de Don Julio*.

We walked slowly, allowing little Victoria to set the pace between us. "Does Victoria like soccer?" I asked.

"She is too young to appreciate it," Sofía said. "But there will be other children there to play with. My friend is bringing her two sons."

We arrived beneath the giant wooden sign hanging from the terrace. The words *Don Julio* were painted in thick, yellow letters, making it impossible to miss. Sofía picked up her daughter and held her with one arm as we climbed the narrow staircase carved between two buildings. At the top was a covered patio, littered with whooping fans, crowded tightly around small, circular tables. They raised their beer

211

bottles high into the air for the final swig and proceeded to wave at the bartender for another round. A bed sheet was hung from the ceiling and used to display the game from a projector.

A lady sitting near the patio raised her arm and waved it wildly, catching Sofía's attention. Sofía recognized her friend and nodded her head in the direction of the table, crossing in front of me as she made her way through the restaurant. The two greeted one another with hugs and proceeded to chitchat as we got situated, making sure to face the screen. Sofía said something in Spanish, causing her friend to giggle and shoot a mischievous grin my way.

"*Mucho gusto*, Mr. Mark," she said, reaching across the table.

"*Encantado*," I said, taking her hand in mine and offering a gentle shake.

Two young boys sat at her side, drawing pictures on napkins. It wasn't long, though, before they grew tired of coloring and began running around the restaurant in a game of tag. The fans were content to let them be. After all, the game had begun and things were starting to get rowdy.

The players kicked and chased the ball across the field, while fans leapt from their seats in a chorus of cheers and commands. With every goal, the cantina erupted. At one point, I could have sworn I heard a gunshot.

I chose a team based on the crowd's response and cheered along. Sofía was happy to return my high-fives, laughing at my sudden interest in a sport that I had, until that day, openly dismissed. Victoria sat quietly, coloring princess pictures in her Disney activity book.

After a few minutes, Victoria closed the book and climbed down from the chair, going straight for her mother's bag. Her short arms disappeared as she dug through the bag, searching for a new activity. At last she reemerged, squeezing a small, illustrated picture book between her fingers. Holding the book straight out from her face, she hurried to her mother's side, presenting the book and begging, "*Mamá! Lea!*" Sofía, hearing her daughter, bent down and pulled Victoria to her lap.

The game was in full swing; fans shouted emphatically throughout the bar. Still, little Victoria had her mother's undivided attention. She opened the book and began reading the story quietly into

Victoria's ear. With each turn of a page, Victoria leaned deeper into Sofía's chest, making herself more and more comfortable.

Sofía's profound love for her child captured me; I couldn't pull my eyes away. Even in the midst of a chaotic soccer game, Sofía would rather comfort and tend to her precious daughter. And for the first time since January, I let go of my bias. Watching Sofía care for Victoria was so attractive; it was downright *sexy*. Before that moment, I'd never given young mothers any romantic thought. Most of the ones I knew were married, and to my shame, the ones that weren't, I had always written off as being too loose in their morals. Now, sitting in a crowded cantina, watching a soccer game with fifty screaming fans, I was forced to reconsider my prejudice.

Little Victoria was not a walking reminder of one moment of weakness in Sofía's life. On the contrary, she was a beautiful human being with a personality and talent and a future. If God wanted me to the a father of a fatherless child, would I be able to set aside my pride and step up to the task? If not in Honduras, then back in the United States?

Victoria decided that she was finished with the story and climbed down from Sofía's lap. She ran across the room to meet the two boys, now lying on the floor and playing with action figures.

"Sofía," I said.

She must have missed it in all the commotion. Resituating herself, she took a drink from her plastic cup and then placed it on the table, resting her hand beside it.

"Sofía," I said again, placing my hand atop hers.

She glanced my direction. I released her hand and pulled it back to my side.

"Sorry," I said. "I was just thinking...well, I dunno. You're just a really good mom."

She smiled. "Thanks."

The game ended and the crowd began to emerge from their seats. Sofía hugged her friend and said goodbye, then turned to me. "She is going to take Victoria for a few hours. Do you want to spend more time in Copán today?"

"Sure," I said. "What do you have in mind?"

"Well, we have to get your cigar," she said. "I do not want you to leave Honduras without doing everything on your list."

Sofía led the way through town as we walked to the only cigar shop either of us knew. Unlike most shops in Copán, this particular store was enclosed in glass windows. There was no question: this was a tourist shop. The bell chimed as we opened the door and walked into the small room. Mahogany shelves full of wooden boxes lined the walls.

"Hello, how are you today?" the clerk offered in English. Sofía and I looked at one another in surprise.

"We're well," I said with a pompous British accent. "Just got in town from London, you know." Sofía said nothing. "Come, darling. Only the best for you."

The clerk seemed surprised at my words, but didn't have a chance to ask any more questions before we walked to the corner and began pointing to fine cigars, discussing them in great detail. Neither of us knew a thing about cigars, except that, if this shop was any indication, they were expensive. I picked up a particularly long cigar with a $50.00 tag taped on and sniffed it from end to end. "Very good, I say," I remarked, handing it to Sofía to do the same. "Which one shall we bring the children?" I asked, taking it back and replacing it on the shelf. Sofía remained silent so as not to spoil the fun with her Spanish accent.

At last I picked up a $5.00 cigar and set it before the clerk. "We've decided," I said.

She blinked rapidly in surprise. "Sir," she began, looking back up at our faces, "If you would like, I will be happy to explain our fine tobacco to you in greater detail."

"No ma'am," I said, holding up my palm. "This will be perfect."

She nodded and typed a few keys into her computer. "That will be $5.00, U.S.," she said.

"Oh, those pesky Americans," I said. "They're so proud of their money. They think it will work anywhere in the world. Here, my dear. I'll make it easy on you." I passed a small handful of lempiras across the counter.

She counted them out and handed back a few bills. "Thank you, sir," she replied, her face flushed. "Enjoy your stay in Copán Ruinas."

214

"I believe we shall," I said, handing the cigar to Sofía, who placed it in her purse. "Let's be off, dearest. We mustn't keep the children waiting."

With that, we left through the front door and exploded into laughter. "At least she has a story now," I said.

"You enjoy giving people stories, don't you?" she asked.

"I'm just trying to pay Honduras back for all the stories it's given me."

Sofía had a place in mind where we could sit and talk as I enjoyed my new souvenir. It was just outside of town, leaving little chance of encountering any students, who would be sure to inform the entire school that Mr. Mark was smoking and Miss Sofía was watching—and what *else* might they have been doing?

"Do you have a lighter?" I asked, as Copán Ruinas shrank into the distance.

"No," she replied. "But I have some matches in my purse."

"That should work," I said. "I mean, I think so. I've never done this before."

"I hope you hate it," Sofía said. I looked at her, puzzled. "I do not want to be the reason that you become addicted to tobacco," she clarified.

I laughed. "I appreciate the sentiment."

We arrived at our destination and took a seat on a fallen tree. We were at the top of a hill overlooking the town. Pine trees surrounded us on all sides, filling the forest with a fragrant aroma. I unwrapped the cigar from its plastic cover and shoved the trash in my pocket. Meanwhile, Sofía pulled the book of matches from her purse and ripped one off. "Are you ready?" she asked. I nodded and held the cigar out. Sofía struck the match and a small flame appeared. She held it to the tip of the cigar just as the fire vanished. Disappointed, we tried again with the same result.

"You have to breathe in when the fire touches the end," she told me.

The third match met the cigar and I inhaled deeply. Nothing but the overbearing scent of tobacco entered my mouth. "Bleh!" I exclaimed.

"Come on, Mark," Sofía said. "Do you want to do this or not? I

215

am running out of matches."

"The flame needs to be bigger," I told her.

"How could the flame be bigger?" she shot back. "This is the size of a match."

We argued for a minute or two and finally resolved to set the entire book on fire.

"We only have one chance to get this right," she said, "So stop being a coward and breathe this time."

"A coward?!"

"Yes, Mark. My grandmother can smoke a cigar better than you."

"Just light the match."

Sofía struck the match and held it to the cardboard flap. Soon, the entire book was engulfed in flame.

"Hurry!" she said. "It is going to burn my hand!"

"Shut up and hold still!"

"Shut up and smoke!"

"Just shut up a second!"

"Shut up! Hurry!"

I brought the cigar to the flame and inhaled deeply. The brown tip turned to ash as a red ring consumed half an inch from the top. I opened my mouth and coughed out a puff of grey smoke. "Boom, baby!" I shouted. "How do you like me now?" Sofía rolled her eyes as I took another whiff. "You can tell your grandma that she's got competition."

Sofía dropped the burning book and stomped out the flame.

For a few minutes, we sat peacefully, watching the busy town in the distance. I occasionally took a puff of the cigar and let out the smoky residue from my mouth.

"You know," I said, holding the cigar out, "this thing sucks." Sofía smiled. I took the half-smoked cigar and smashed the tip on a rock, putting out the burn.

"What do you want to do now?" she asked.

"I've got about an hour before the last bus to Oranado," I said. "Let's get coffee."

"Coffee?" Sofía tilted her head back slightly and squinted at me. "I thought men and women only get coffee together when they want to— how did you say— 'get to know each other'."

"Well, maybe I want to get to know you," I said, offering my hand to help her off the tree.

She took it and stood to her feet. Our hands didn't part, though. Instead, our fingers gently slipped between the others' and grasped firmly. Her eyes locked onto mine as our faces inched closer and closer, until our eyes closed and our lips met.

Chapter 28
Café Hondureño

Sofía's face slowly pulled away. I kept my eyes closed for a few more seconds, then opened them with a smile and whispered, "*Hola*."

"*Hola*," she giggled, her eyes squinting as she smiled.

"So, um, you still wanna get coffee?"

"Yes," she nodded, releasing my hand to lift her purse from the ground.

We arrived at Café San Rafael and ordered two *café negros*. Walking to the table in the back, I set the mugs down and pulled out a chair for Sofía. Taking a seat myself, I went straight for the sugar jar in the center of the table.

"Do you need sugar for your coffee?" Sofía asked, as I dipped my spoon into the brown crystals.

I looked up. "Yeah, it's a little too strong for me."

"Oh, that is too bad," Sofía said, taking the mug with both hands and bringing it to her lips.

"You know what?" I said, pulling my empty spoon out of the jar and setting it on the table. "Sugar doesn't sound good today." I held the mug to my mouth and took a sip, forcing myself to swallow, then stuck out my tongue in sheer disgust. "Ok, I give up. Pass me the sugar," I said, taking off the glass lid and dumping the brown crystals straight into my coffee.

Sofía laughed. "*Gringos*," she said, shaking her head. She took another sip and sat the mug down. "So what do you talk about when you get coffee with a girl?" she asked.

"Well," I thought aloud, "Usually we'd talk about work and school — you know, just finding out what each other's lives are like. Then we might get deeper and ask what each other's plans are when life allows us to move on. Sometimes we talk about our dreams for the future. If things are going really well, we might talk about the past."

"Shouldn't the past come first?" Sofía asked.

"Yeah, I guess that would make sense," I said. "But usually the past is the most private part of our lives. We are the way we are because of the things we've gone through. The more you find out about someone's past, the more you understand them now."

Sofía was silent for a moment. "That makes sense, I suppose" she finally said, lifting her coffee and lightly blowing the steam away.

"We can start somewhere else if you want," I said. "There's no, like, 'Coffee Shop Constitution' or whatever. We both know how work and school are going since we both work at the same school."

Sofía smiled. "Ok, so what are your plans for the future?"

I swallowed my sugar-smothered coffee, then exhaled and sat the mug down. "I've got a few more weeks here and then I'm headed home. I guess I'll just start working somewhere. Maybe go back to college and finish my bachelor's degree."

"What will you study in college?" she asked.

"Who knows? Maybe Spanish or something," I said. "I've got an associate's, but I really need a bachelor's before I can do anything important."

"*Anything important*?" Sofía repeated. "What do you mean?"

"You know, like being a real teacher or a social worker or a journalist," I explained. "Something that allows me to make more money than I would without an education."

Sofía looked down at the table and blinked a few times.

"Something the matter?" I asked.

"Gringos are just...different," she said.

"How so?"

"You think that you are 'important' because of what job you have or how much money you make," she said. "Most people here do not even finish high school, and almost no one is rich. For us, there is nothing more important than family."

I couldn't argue. I stared down at the dark, steaming drink before me and circled the rim with my finger. "What are your dreams, Sofía?" I asked.

"Me? Oh, I do not have many dreams for myself. I want to give Victoria the best life I can. That is my only goal. I used to have many dreams when I was younger. I wanted to go to the U.S. and study in university."

"Did you ever try?" I brought my eyes back to her face.

"Yes, of course," she said. "I had all of the papers ready. I knew exactly where I wanted to go. I even had money saved up for my passport and visa. But when I went to the Immigration Office in San Pedro, they told me to go home. I asked why they would not see me, but they did not give me an answer."

"Wait," I interjected. "You're telling me that you tried to come to the U.S. *legally* and they wouldn't even let you *start* the process?"

"Yes," she said, staring hard into my eyes. "The system is not fair, Mark. Not for us. This is why many Honduran people go to the U.S. illegally, like José is going to do very soon."

I shook my head, remembering the Immigration Office in San Pedro Sula only a couple months ago. It *was* unfair. All of it. What difference did I have from these people besides my place of birth?

"I'm sorry, Sofía," I offered, having no other consolation. "Are you ever going to try again?"

"I have tried three times," she said. "But now, how can I? I have Victoria to take care of."

"Where is Victoria's father?" I asked, immediately realizing that I may have overstepped my bounds. Fidgeting with a salt packet, I tried frantically to think of another question, but before I could, Sofía answered.

"I do not know. He did not want to be a father, so he left."

I dropped the packet on the table and stared at her in disbelief. "Sofía, I am so sorry."

"No, it is a good thing," she said. "He never would have loved Victoria the way she deserves. And how can I be mad? He is a man. Why should I expect him to respect me?"

"I don't understand," I said, perplexed.

Sofía sighed. "Mark, you are very kind and I enjoy my time with you, but even you must know that men are dogs. They cannot be trusted. They only want sex. And once they are done, they move on to the next woman."

I had no words. Sofía was completely serious. She continued. "Before Victoria was born, I discovered that her father was cheating on me. I asked my mother what I should do and she said to me, 'Sofía, men will never be faithful. You must accept that fact if you ever want to be happy.' I did not believe her at first, but over the years, I have learned that she was right."

Silence followed. I looked intently at Sofía's face, for the first time seeing stains from years of bitterness at every crease. In that moment, something changed. No longer did I see a cute, carefree girl waiting to be swept off her feet by Yours Truly. In her place sat a strong, independent woman, carrying the scars of betrayal, rejection, and hurt.

I finally broke the tension, "Sofía... I'm sorry you've been hurt so many times. I realize there's nothing I can say to make you change your mind. But I can tell you that I completely disagree with what you said, and not because I think I'm better than the other guys. I've just seen so many marriages work."

Now it was Sofía's turn to sit in silence as I told story after story of the married men and women back home. I told her of Phil and Christine, who, after fifty years of marriage, had never had a fight, instead considering the other more important than their own pride; of Nate and Tracy, parents of four, who still managed to find the time to mentor and love college students at their church while loving their kids and each other; of Rob and Denise, who suffered through an affair, fought for reconciliation, forgave one another, and found themselves more in love than they ever had been before.

"But how are those things even possible?" Sofía interjected. "Why is it so easy for those people?"

"I don't think it's *easy*," I said. "I think the reason it worked for them is because they decided to stay together, even in the hard times. I think it would have probably been easier to leave."

"But why would anyone choose the hard way?" Sofía asked as her eyes glazed over.

"Because, they all have one thing in common," I answered. "All of those people I told you about, they all know Jesus. Gah, that sounds so churchy and dumb. But it's *true*. All of those husbands and wives, they take the Bible seriously when it says that they should love each other like Jesus loves the Church. Jesus *died* for the Church. I don't think *that* was an easy decision, but it shows us how deeply we should love each other."

By now, tears were streaming down Sofía's face.

"Can I ask you a really honest question?"

She nodded.

"What do you think about Jesus?"

"Huh?"

"Well, Jesus did all these good things and taught us to love each other and all. Nobody really argues that. But if the Bible is true, then Jesus is God—like, really, actually *God*. And if he is, then that means that all that stuff Jesus did and said about love, that's God; he loves us. Do you believe that?"

She brought her hand to her face, wiping her wet cheeks and took a breath. After a moment of composure, she shrugged and said, "I think so. I used to."

"What changed?" I asked.

"I was part of a—how do you say when teenagers go to church?"

"Youth group?"

"Yes, a youth group in Santa Rosa. I felt so close to God. Everyone was kind and acted like they really loved me. Then one day we discovered that the pastor was sleeping with another woman in the church. He said that he no longer believed in God and he divorced his wife to be with his new lover. After that, many people began to admit that they were sleeping with other people in the church. A lot of them said that they no longer knew what they believed in. Many of my friends became *ateos*—atheists. That was when I stopped going to church." She sighed. "If there is a God, and he loves us, why does he let things like this happen?"

My eyes were glued to Sofía as her layers were peeled back before my eyes. What could I possibly say to mend her heart?

I sighed and dropped my hands onto the table. "Sofía, I...I don't know. I have *no idea*. Trust me, I wish I did. All I know is that it sucks. It sucks that bad things happen. It sucks that people cheat on their partners. It sucks that some people never get the chance to follow their dreams. It sucks that men can run away from the responsibilities of parenthood and women have to do twice as much work to raise their kids. I...God, I just don't know.

"There are so many people—people I know—who *never* have

223

doubts. It's like believing in God is the easiest thing in the world for them. And I don't get that. Faith, for me, is really, *really* hard. And I think sometimes the Church makes it harder than it needs to be. For years, I followed a long list of rules, because I thought my faith had to be, like, *perfect* to be a real Christian.

"But when I read the stories in the Bible about Jesus, that's not the person I see."

Sofía was silent. I continued. "Jesus didn't run around condemning gay people or promoting national pride or belittling people for their beliefs about the age of the earth. He went straight to the 'worst' people in society—the ones who were hated and rejected and left outside to die in the shadows. And he loved on those people; you know, he got dirty, he faced public ridicule, got kicked out of religious institutions. He helped a lot of people, sure, but he didn't save the world by overthrowing the government. He saved it by suffering. That's the Jesus I want to know—not the other one."

She leaned in.

"I don't claim to know it all, Sofía. Honestly, I don't claim to know anything for sure. Sometimes—*most* times—I wonder the same things you do. Your questions are legitimate, and you have the right to ask them. Trust me, I understand. I was ready to let go, to walk away and never look back. But for some reason, I didn't. Maybe...I dunno...maybe I should have. But I didn't. And I'm kind of glad.

"I've lost so much in the last few months. But the few things I've found, well, they've changed my life. Things are so screwed up in this world. But I think that God—if there is a God—I think he's good—like, really, actually *good*."

Sofía's eyes had dried. She sat expressionless as I spoke, occasionally nodding to affirm that I had her attention.

"Do you own a Bible?" I asked.

"Yes," she said, "but I never read it."

"You should try," I told her. "Things didn't *really* change for me until I started reading the Psalms and being honest about my doubts and questions." I gave her a moment, then said, "Would you be willing to give it a try?"

She nodded. "Yes," she answered, just above a whisper. "But I do not know the Bible like you. Where do I even begin?"

"How about with Jesus?"

She thought hard for a few seconds, then met my eyes. "Ok."

We agreed to start in Matthew and work our way forward, reading one chapter a day and discuss it the next day. She promised to bring questions and verses that she found surprising, interesting, or upsetting, and I would do the same.

Neither of us finished our coffee; it had gone cold.

"Thank you for listening, Mark," she said, gathering her belongings as she stood up and pushed in the chair.

"Thank you for being so honest with me," I said, following suit.

Sofía walked around the table and met me with open arms. I closed my eyes and held her close. I wouldn't kiss her, though. Not now. Something had changed. Sofía didn't need a boyfriend. She needed time, space, healing. It wouldn't be easy to set aside my feelings. I wanted her. But more than that, I wanted restoration *for* her.

God...just...just...take care of her. Please.

We left Café San Rafael and walked side by side toward the plaza. Puffy, grey clouds blocked out the sun, threatening a downpour at any moment. A low rumble fell from the sky and echoed through the streets.

"I doubt I'm getting home before this storm hits," I said, as we reached the corner where we would go our separate ways.

"Probably not," she said.

We looked at one another in silence. Then I spoke.

"Sofía, I like you."

"I like you, Mark," she agreed with a half-smile.

"Maybe now isn't the best time to start something, though."

She nodded, keeping her expression. "Yes," she said. "I agree."

"But we should still, you know, hang out."

Her smile grew just enough to trigger that squint. "I like that idea."

"I guess I'll see you on Monday," I said.

"As long as you stay alive until then," she added with a full smile.

I laughed. "So, um, how do we do this? Like, shake hands or something?" I extended my right hand awkwardly.

Sofía rolled her eyes, then threw her arms around me and squeezed. "You are *such* a dumb gringo," she said.

Fat raindrops fell sporadically from the sky, slapping the ground in every direction. Sofía pulled away. "*Adios, amigo!* See you Monday!" She held her purse above her head and darted down the road.

I watched her shrink into the distance as the rain soaked my clothes. "*Adios amiga*," I whispered with a smile. "I'm looking forward to it."

PART SIX

receiving

Chapter 29

The First Goodbye

With every passing day, school drew nearer to its end. June 19 was approaching at an increasingly rapid pace. The sun stayed out later those days, but would spend a few hours hiding behind enormous thunderheads. Rainy Season was in full swing. Every day at 4:30, just like clockwork, the cloudy dams burst open and slammed the entire country with rain for an hour. Then, just as quickly as it had started, the storm came to an abrupt end, leaving only the flooded streets and bleak overcast as evidence. In a matter of minutes, the clouds vanished entirely, allowing the sun to make up for lost time by torturing its victims with relentless humidity.

Some days even saw two or three storms. Not one day passed, however, that the entire town of Oranado didn't completely lose power. While this forced me to reset my alarm clock at least once a day, it also provided hours of entertainment in my hammock, watching the lightning crackle behind the mountains. The sound of raindrops on tin roofs accompanied the afternoon's album of choice.

Nights were cooler during Rainy Season. I started falling asleep in my hammock on a regular basis. I'd sleep as late as I could before Lora decided it was time to notify the town that the sun was up. I found that my mood drastically improved on nights I'd slept outside—all the better, as time with my students was drawing to a close.

In those final days, I spent the majority of class time preparing the students for their final exams. The Honduran Board of Education implemented certain requirements for every student, and final exams played an enormous role. If a student didn't pass, they wouldn't be moving on to the next grade. As my students were at the age when Honduran kids generally dropped out of school, it was of the utmost importance that they passed their finals. It was the only way to guarantee they kept trying.

By the time finals week arrived, my students knew the material

231

well enough to could quote it in two languages while sleeping. With finals only a day away, I decided it was time for a break. They had earned it. After all, once finals were over, so would be our time together.

The sixth graders were happy to spend the day chatting with one another. One girl brought an art set to class, full of glitter and markers. Most of the girls shared supplies with one another, writing letters to boys in the school to confess their hidden love. The boys, on the other hand, spoke of nothing but the upcoming World Cup in Brazil, flipping through sports magazines and idolizing the players.

Somehow, the idea that children are more grateful for their education in third world countries had crept into my mind before coming to Honduras. 2014 had certainly disproved that theory. It was a lesson sorely learned over six months. Even so, one thing remained constant: kids will always be kids, no matter what country they come from.

Seventh grade was different: had I left them to their own devices, they would have burned down the school. Walking to the front of the room, I shouted, in my best game show announcer voice, "Welcome to the Seventh Grade Award Show!" The students were confused, but it never took much to get them excited. They began clapping and cheering wildly. I gestured for them to a bring it down just a notch.

Reaching into my backpack, I pulled out the first object I could find: a paperclip. "The first award goes to none other than Filipe!" Filipe stood up and took a bow, as the cheers reemerged. "Filipe gets the award for best handwriting!" Filipe made his way to the front and took the paper clip. "Would you like to say anything, Filipe?" I asked. He thought for a moment, then shrugged. "No." And with that, he sat back down at his desk to even more applause.

I shuffled through my backpack again, this time pulling out a pencil. "The next award goes to Kiara, for taking the most bathroom breaks!" Kiara stood to her feet with an enormous grin as she came to collect her award.

The rest of class time was spent passing out trinkets from my backpack and presenting them to students as personalized awards. Each student received wild applause and laughter as their specific award was announced. By the end, my backpack had lost almost as much weight as I had.

"Mee-stair, what about *your* award?" Josué called from the back.

"Yes! You must have one!" students shouted from every direction.

"Guys, I can't give *myself* an award," I said.

"I will give you an award," Valeria said, hopping out of her chair before I could stop her. She ran to the whiteboard and pulled the cap off of a red marker. In giant letters, she wrote *Mr. Mark* and underlined it. Beneath, she began a list:

Nice

Funny

Happy

Students began shouting suggestions, which Valeria added to the list:

Gives good high fives
Likes to sing Taylor Swift
No more fat
Good English
Terrible haircut

At last, she pushed the cap back onto the marker and placed it on the metal tray beneath the board, skipping gleefully back to her desk. I looked at the list and smiled. Over the applause came a shout: "Say something, Mee-stair!"

I turned around to face the students. "Well," I began, "you guys weren't always the easiest class to control." A few rowdy students nudged one another, snickering. "But," I continued, "I've really enjoyed being your teacher this year. And, well, I hope you've enjoyed teaching me too."

The class erupted into cheers just as the bell signaled the end of class. I walked to the door, but was stopped short by a multitude of students holding up their hands for high-fives.

"Yeah, Mee-stair! You are great! We love you!"

I may never teach again. But there's no better way it could have

233

ended.

Four blank stares greeted me as I walked into eighth grade.

"Please, Mee-stair," Sara begged, "We do not want to study anymore. We know everything about the exam."

"Well, what would you like to do today instead?" I said, removing my backpack and placing it on the front desk.

"We could play soccer," suggested Rodrigo.

"With five people?" Then an idea hit me. "Actually, why don't we go ahead and spend the day on the soccer court? Martín, will you go to the office and meet us on the court with a basketball?"

He looked confused, but obeyed without an argument. They would gladly take an outdoor activity over more studying.

We walked down the stairs to the paved soccer court and sat in the shadow of the wall. Martín arrived with the basketball and passed it to me, then joined his classmates on the concrete bleachers.

"Have you guys ever heard of the game PIG?" I asked, dribbling the ball.

The students stared back, expressionless.

"PIG," I repeated. "You know, like *cerdo*?"

"Yes, Mee-stair!" spouted Sara. "We are not stupid. We know what means *pig*."

"Fair enough," I said. "Well, back in the U.S., we play a game with a basketball called PIG." I quickly explained the basics of the game. "Does all that make sense?" I asked.

"Yes, of course, Mee-stair!" Abril said, rolling her eyes.

"Alright, Shaquille O'Neal," I said, passing her the ball. "Game on."

The game was a huge success. The kids loved scoring against one another and attempting impossible shots. I didn't win one game. They especially enjoyed that.

When at last Abril made the final basket, putting me out for the third consecutive time, she threw her arms in the air and circled the court, screaming, "Oh yeah! I am the best!"

"You're the best," I said, offering a five. "Hey guys, let's head back to the room to get ready for Miss Donna's class."

Abril tossed the ball my direction and joined her classmates moving toward the stairs. I followed behind, dribbling the ball to the edge of the court and placing it beneath my arm to climb the staircase.

"Mee-stair, are you coming?" Martín shouted from the classroom door.

"I'm just gonna drop the ball off in the office," I called back. Then, turning around, I nearly crashed into the person walking my direction. "Oh, I'm sorry! Uh, *perdón! Perdón!*"

The face that met me wasn't upset or flustered. Rather, it was somber, almost sad.

"Woah, are you good, man?" José asked.

"Yeah," I said. "I'm just headed this way to put the ball up. I guess I didn't see you there."

"Well, I am glad we ran into each other."

"Yeah? What's up?"

He sighed. "I am leaving."

"Oh, you're heading out early? Is something wrong?"

"No, man," he said, looking me directly in the eyes. "It is time."

"It's only 1:00. We still have a couple more classes to go."

"Yes, but *I* am finished. I just came from the office."

And it hit me. The day had finally come. Tomorrow José would set out on a new path—one shrouded in uncertainty. I nodded in silence, then put out my hand. His hand met mine and squeezed tightly.

"Be careful up there, man," I said.

"Of course," he answered. "And you be careful down here."

"Always."

José snickered. "Yeah right, man. I can read you like a book."

We both laughed.

"I'll be praying for you," I said. It was a phrase I had used innumerable times before. But this time, I meant it. Not a day would pass when I wouldn't ask God to keep José safe, give him success, and cover him with peace.

José smiled through his solemn expression. "Do not worry, man," he said. "God is going to take care of everything."

He released my hand and walked down the stairs, through the

open field, past the gate, and disappeared behind the trees along the road.

Chapter 30

Bonfire

When I started reading my Bible in Honduras, I found myself drawn to David— the guy who wrote most of the Psalms. The more time I spent in the gospels, however, the more I began to see my reflection in another prominent Biblical figure. His name was Peter.

Like David, Peter was always reacting to his emotions. More often than not, it landed him in trouble. Peter's faith was once so strong and so sure that he willingly jumped out of a boat into a deep, stormy sea, and walked atop the surface. No sooner had his feet met the water than he began to reconsider his decision and promptly sank into the sea. Jesus yanked him up and helped him into the boat, saying, "Peter, why did you doubt?"

Then there was the time that Jesus predicted his death and Peter pulled him aside to rebuke him. Yes, Peter actually *rebuked* Jesus Christ. "Stop, Jesus. You're saying things you don't mean. Just shut up a second and think about what you mean to say." When I read that, I couldn't believe it. Peter actually thought he knew what was better for Jesus than Jesus did. To Peter's horror, Jesus shouted, "Get behind me, Satan!" I imagine that must've stung.

The story that gets me every time, though, is the Transfiguration. In chapter nine of Luke's Gospel, we're given the story of Jesus pulling aside three disciples—Peter, James, and John—to take a trip up a mountain together. Once they arrive at the summit, Jesus starts praying, and in a few minutes, he becomes incandescently bright and indescribably beautiful. Moses and Elijah decide to join the party from Heaven, and soon the three amigos are chatting up a storm.

Peter, James, and John wake up from their naps to see the spectacle, and—rightfully so—they flip out. Somebody should probably say something, right? This is a once-in-a-lifetime opportunity. So our boy, Peter, decides to take the responsibility upon himself. What follows are the most obvious, self-evident, thoughtless words ever uttered by human lips in the history of mankind:

"Master, it is good for us to be here."

Astute observation, Captain Obvious.

There are moments in the Biblical narrative when I have a hard time understanding a character's motivation. Why did Sarah laugh at God, knowing full well that he was listening? Why did Japheth sacrifice his own daughter after a successful battle? Why did Jesus curse a fig tree just because it wouldn't bear fruit?

But Peter's line in Luke chapter nine takes the cake.

Peter had a front row seat to the most hallowed event he would ever see. Scripture was fulfilled before his eyes. He sat in the very presence of the Holy Incarnate Christ in his truest form, speaking to the greatest saints in Hebrew history. And the only thing he could think to say was, "It is good for us to be here." Of course it was! Hey, guess what, Peter? Water is wet! Grass is green! Never had I so desperately wanted to open-palm slap a grown man in the face before (albeit 2000 years too late).

I expressed these frustrations with Sofía over coffee. "Peter is such an idiot! I just can't believe *that's* what he said."

She rolled her eyes. "You would not have said anything better if you were there."

"Whatever!" I shot back. "I could come up with a thousand things on the spot. I would ask Jesus if this is what everyone in Heaven looks like, and I would ask Moses and Elijah questions about their lives that the Bible leaves out. I might even ask for an autograph. And I would definitely ask Jesus why he brought me up the mountain to see him like this."

"You honestly believe that you would be thinking all of those things while Jesus was in his true form?" Sofía pressed.

"I told you, I've started questioning everything over the last six months," I said, taking a swig of coffee. "I think Jesus would answer my questions."

"Then why did God ignore Peter?" she replied.

"What do you mean?"

"Peter wanted to build tents for Jesus and the Saints, right?"

"Right…"

"But God said, 'This is my son. Listen to him.'"

"Sure."

"God did not give any attention to Peter's idea."

"So what's your point?"

"My point," she explained, "is that God did not care about Peter's ideas that day. He only wanted Peter to be quiet and listen to Jesus."

"Yeah, ok, but why?"

"Why what?"

"Why wouldn't God talk to Peter and answer his question? I mean, granted, it was a *stupid* question…"

Sofía sighed loudly, then said, "Mark, you know the Bible better than I do, but I think you are missing the point this time. Maybe when Peter saw Jesus like this, nothing else mattered; nothing else seemed good except Jesus. Maybe Peter was not as stupid as you think, and maybe God did not *want* to answer his questions in that moment. Maybe he just wanted Peter to worship Jesus, because Jesus was enough."

Who was this woman? Her interpretation made sense—lots of sense. Still, I'd spent the night angry at Peter, and I wasn't ready to concede just yet. I took another sip of coffee, allowing the emotional dust to settle. Finally, setting my mug onto the table, I exhaled and acknowledged the elephant in the room.

"Tomorrow's my last full day in Honduras."

Sofía took a drink as well. "I am going to miss you when you are gone," she said.

"You know, I didn't think I would feel this way," I said. "I'm ready to be home, for sure, but I'm really going to miss all of this once I'm gone. I'll definitely miss having these talks with you."

She nodded. We watched silently as a hummingbird swooped down to the flowers on the windowsill and hovered over them. Then, just as quickly as it had appeared, it was gone. Our eyes met across the table once again.

"What are you going to do tomorrow?" Sofía asked.

I shook my head and shrugged. "Probably the same thing I do every day: walk around Copán one last time, get some coffee, lay in my hammock. Nothing fancy."

A smile began to grow on Sofía's face—first in her eyes, then inching up from her lips to her soft cheeks. "Let's do something fancy, then," she said.

I smiled back. "What do you have in mind?"

"Let's go to Alta Vista again," she said. "We can look at the stars from the mountaintop. Maybe we can have a bonfire. The children would love it."

I couldn't deny that I was enticed by the idea. Even if I hadn't been, Sofía's smile was enough to hold me ransom.

"Alright," I said. "Let's do that."

I stayed at Café San Rafael while Sofía went home to gather a few necessities for the evening. She reappeared with a backpack and little Victoria, and we made for the bus station. When we arrived in Oranado, I made a quick trip to the house to grab a few things of my own. We bought two bottles of water from a nearby *pulperia* and began our trek up the mountain. There were no arrangements made for our overnight stay, but the memory of the townspeople's kindness on our adventure to *el salto* gave us hope.

The hike took longer than last time. We took turns carrying Victoria when the walk became too strenuous for her tiny legs, and stopped to rest more than a few times. The views were just as magnificent as ever. We passed by the mountaintop soccer field, now completely vacant, and finally reached the sharp turn in the road, passing out of sight behind the trees. We had arrived.

As soon as the children spotted us, they began pouring from their homes to meet us in the street. Though they had enjoyed nearly a week of Summer Break so far, they were thrilled to see our faces again. They immediately began making plans for the evening. We would ride horses and have relay races and roast marshmallows over a fire.

"This was a great idea," I told Sofía as we walked downhill into town. "You're a genius."

She didn't say anything, but *I know* was written all over her face.

The kids kept each of their promises. Every activity was quickly followed by the next, allowing for only a few minutes of rest in between. The sky slowly faded from blue to orange as the sun steadily sank beneath the curved horizon. About that time, we were called into a small house. An elderly lady—the grandmother of a good number of the children in town—had prepared coffee and homemade bread. Sofía and I entered the cramped dining room and sat at the table as the kids piled in around us.

We drank coffee, ate bread, told jokes, sang songs... but mostly, we laughed. And as the laughter grew, so did the group. Families came out from their homes to join the festivities, some standing outside the house and others crowding around the table. It was chaos—in the best possible way.

"Sofía," I whispered into her ear as the crowd roared, "I'll be back in a little bit."

She cocked her head to look at me, and asked, "Where are you going?"

"I'm just going for a short walk," I told her. "Don't worry. I won't go far."

She wasn't convinced, but hesitantly scooted forward, giving me just enough room to slip by. I left the house and headed up the road.

The call of the mountains was overwhelming, and the sunset only amplified their voice. These opportunities were dwindling with each passing minute. In a matter of hours, I would be back in southwest Missouri, longing to see God's handiwork from the mountaintops.

I retraced our steps down the dirt road, until Alta Vista had disappeared from sight. Far below, I could see the tiny town of Oranado nestled between the mountains. *Where am I even going? Just don't get killed—not this close to the end.* Then, almost immediately, I found my destination: the mountaintop soccer field.

Leaving the road behind, I hiked across the plain and took a seat on a slump in the short grass. The sky blushed a bright pink, painting the trees and rocks for miles in every direction. I was nothing more than an insect on the leaf of a tree in a vast forest called Planet Earth. And in that knowledge, I sat in silence, taking it all in.

I was reminded of my first week in Honduras—my long hike into uncharted territory, into the village. I smiled, recalling my fear as the machete-man led me down the mountain in the dark, and my relief when I made it home safely.

I thought of Marlon, and wondered what he was doing at that moment. Praying? Eating with his family? Hosting a stranger in his home? I could vividly recall the taste of the soup on my tongue, and the fullness in my heart when I watched his family wave goodbye.

I thought about José, and realized that he'd be closer to Missouri now than I was. What faith that man had. José had taught me so much about hospitality, trust, sacrifice, and even the foundations of a new language. What would my time have been without his kindness?

I thought of all the help that I, an American, had received from so many people in Honduras—the tourism group at the Guatemalan border; the British couple in Copán; my American counterpart, Donna; of Aaron and his family in Florida; my parents; the church that raised the money to send the books; my Canadian friends, David and Shelly; of Enrique, and even Hissela. Each of these people had played a critical role in keeping me safe, legal, and sane.

I thought about the faces of my friends back home, whom I would see in only a few short days. Even from so far away, they had sacrificed their time and energy to keep up with and encourage me. I remembered that fateful Sunday morning, how they'd prayed for me, and how, for two wonderful hours, they'd transported me home.

I thought of my students, most of whom I would surely never see again. They had worked hard to overcome the odds in a place where most students drop out by sixth grade. I fervently hoped they would finish, and finish strong. My part in their stories was complete. The rest would be out of my hands.

I thought about all the ridiculous hurdles I had faced in such a short period: I'd been dumped, my bank account hacked, I'd nearly missed my last chance to leave the country legally, I'd faced deportation because of a simple U.S. Customs mistake, I had acquired a tropical disease that landed me in a hospital. Yet, here I was, healthy, legal, and financially stable.

I thought about Sofía. I could so clearly hear her story in my mind. She was strong—stronger than I could have ever hoped to be at twenty-five. So much hurt, so much confusion, so much betrayal. But somewhere deep, there was a spark—the same spark I carried in my heart, perpetually igniting a yearning to know and be known by a loving Heavenly Father. I knew it was there; I'd seen it.

And then I stopped thinking altogether and simply watched the sky. Should I pray? Sing? Write? There were just no words to convey the goodness, the creativity, the beauty, the mystery, the silence, the friendship, the love... the still, small voice of God.

"Jesus," I whispered, "It's good for me to be here."

And for the first time in six months, I stopped asking questions and let him be enough.

Six months earlier, my life was permanently changed. June seemed well beyond any foreseeable future. The only thing I could determine from my lonely January vantage point was that by the time June did roll around, I'd have either encountered God in an unmistakable fashion, securing my faith forevermore, or I'd have abandoned it completely, seeing the world for the first time in my life through the eyes of atheism.

June came.

And neither happened.

Jesus hadn't appeared in a glorious blinding light, but neither had he abandoned me to my own despair in a meaningless, Godless cosmos. And so I was stuck in the middle. There would be no *proof* of a living God. How could there be? In a world where science continued to fill the gaps, the need for God was shrinking daily. And yet, if there *was* a God—a God who loves his children, who suffers with the hurting, who longs to see the world made right, who lives not *over* his people, but *among* them—if there was any chance of a God like that, I just couldn't abandon the hope in my heart, even amidst the doubt in my head.

"Every head bowed; every eye closed," I'd heard from countless preachers. "God knows what you're thinking! Tonight, you'd better *know* that you *know* that you *know* that you *know* that God is real, and that Jesus is his son!"

243

I used to know. Not anymore.

Hope, though, is strong. And if hope was enough to keep Peter and David coming back to God, even on their worst days, when doubt and despair plagued their minds and eclipsed their hearts, then maybe it would be enough for me too.

The bonfire was held in the center of town that night. It brought out kids and adults alike, as only a fire can do. The boys took turns leaping over the flames to impress the girls. The rest of us stood to the side, holding out sticks with punctured marshmallows and hotdogs over the heat, reminiscing about our favorite moments of the year.

When the fire died down and the festivities drew to an end, Sofía and I were invited into a house with two spare bedrooms. Before walking through the door, I peeked upward to the sky. A million stars silently sang a spectacular lullaby from the heavens—more than I had ever seen.

It was a perfect night, through and through; a perfect ending to an adventure that was anything but perfect.

But maybe that was the point.

Chapter 31

The Last Goodbye

Bvvvt-bvvvvvvvvt

Bvvvt-bvvvvvvvvt

BVVVT-BVVVT-BVVVVVVVVT

Ignoring the alarm that morning wasn't an option. It was the day I'd been waiting for since January. Tempting though it was to simply lie in my hammock and watch the sun slowly rise over the mountains, I knew there wasn't time. If I didn't get up now, I'd have to skip a shower. This day was going to be long, and a shower wasn't a sacrifice I was willing to make. Still, after six months of readjusting to a new culture, nothing felt as earned as those few extra minutes admiring the beauty of the country I had come to know so well.

All of my clothes and belongings had been neatly packed away in two purple suitcases. Over the last few weeks I had given away many of my possessions. The shampoo and towel I would use that morning had found their permanent home in Central America, along with my desk fan, hammock, and a handful of books.

Turning the knob to the shower and stepping beneath the faucet, I ran my hands through my short hair. The water was ice cold, but I was hardly fazed. Showers used to take no less than twenty minutes; I'd jump in and out of the water, pep-talking myself to completion each time. Now I stood directly in the stream and washed myself in less than five minutes without so much as a shiver.

A pair of jeans and a soccer jersey were laid out at the foot of the bed. I slipped them on as Lora began her morning announcement: "MOMMY!" I dragged my bags through the garden, one by one, to the *pulperia* and set them by the open door. Hissela's sisters greeted me

245

from behind the counter. They had been awake for hours, preparing for another long day of work.

A rusty, grey pickup truck caught my eye as it raced by the door. I stepped outside onto the sidewalk and breathed in the crisp morning air. The truck drove down the street, cutting through the intersection, and onto the dirt road trailing up the mountain to Alta Vista. Less than twenty-four hours ago, I had told Sofía goodbye at that very spot.

"So I'll meet you in Copán at 11:00?" I had said, hopping out of the truck at the intersection.

"Yes," she answered. "At Café San Rafael. Our table."

"Sounds perfect," I said with a smile. I gave the tailgate a double-pat and the driver sped off toward Copán. Sofía, surrounded by children, kept my stare all the way down the road, until the truck rounded the corner and she was gone.

A quick shower and a change of clothes later, I was on a bus headed to Copán. I ran to Café San Rafael, making it with ten minutes to spare, then sat down at our table in the back and watched the door.

A lot of people walked through that door over the next hour. But Sofía wasn't one of them. I waited and waited. But she never came.

I tried to shrug it off, to convince myself that it wasn't a big deal—that the excitement to be home outweighed the pain of being abandoned by a dear friend. Try as I may, though, I couldn't stop thinking about her. She had been my last thought before sleeping and my first thought upon waking up. And although I knew she must have had a good reason, it didn't make that final morning any easier.

I stood outside the doorway in the quiet street, drinking in the last few drops of warm sunrise. Donna joined me soon thereafter, laying her bags at the door beside mine. Hissela walked into the *pulperia* and bid us good morning from inside. She told us that breakfast was ready in the kitchen and that she had something for each of us to take back to the United States.

Breakfast consisted of eggs, refried beans, plantains, and tortillas. As we ate, Hissela presented us with her parting gifts. To Donna, she gave a book with some special significance between the two of them. Donna loved it, thanking her again and again. To me, she gave seven bags of Honduran coffee.

"I know you like the coffee here," she said.

"I do," I agreed, holding a silver bag in my hand to admire it. "Thank you."

Donna slid her empty plate forward and slowly stood to her feet. "Well, I better go downstairs and make sure I have everything," she said. "I'd hate to get back to Virginia and realize I'd forgotten something."

She lightly pushed in her chair and made for the stairs. I shoved one last plantain slice into my mouth and stood to follow.

"Mark," Hissela said.

I turned around, placing my hands on the chair back. "Hmm?" I offered, swallowing my bite.

"I wanted to speak with you privately before we leave for the airport."

Oh no.

"This year has not been easy—for either of us, I presume."

I nodded.

"There has been a lot of tension in the last month. Would you agree?"

"Yeah," I said. "I would agree."

"I have hosted many American teachers at Santa Lucia," she said. "But I have never worried about them as much as I have worried for you. You have a free spirit. I admire that. But I also worry that it will kill you someday."

She took a sip of water, then placed the glass back onto the table. "This is your last day in Honduras, and since you are still alive, I suppose I can finally stop worrying." She scanned the table with her eyes and sighed, bringing her gaze back to mine. "The children loved you, Mark. And for that, I am glad you came to teach at Santa Lucia. I know you worked very hard this year. I have seen it. I want to thank you for that."

I nodded lightly. "Thank you," I said, just above a whisper. "It means a lot."

"I hope, some day, you will come back," she said.

And I think she actually meant it.

We drove in silence through the mountains that morning. Thick fog hovered over the roads, forcing Hissela to drive slowly around corners and through small towns. The fog came to an abrupt halt just before the mountain range reached its end. I looked back at the wall of cloud that veiled the rugged country behind it, nodding silently—a final parting gesture to an old friend.

The road began to level out and the traffic grew heavier, until at last we merged onto the highway. When we arrived at San Pedro Sula International Airport, Donna and I pulled our bags from the Jeep and walked inside.

We checked our luggage and stood in line at the bank to pay the travel tax. Hissela parked the Jeep and met us inside to make sure everything was in order.

"I think I have everything situated," Donna said.

"Yeah, me too," I added.

"Well then," Hissela said, "be safe in your travels." She looked at me and raised one eyebrow.

"Thank you," Donna said.

I nodded. "Thanks," I said with a half smile.

"I suppose it is time, then," she said.

She hugged each of us and stood watching as we presented our passports at the gate and made our way up the escalator. Looking back one last time, I offered a wave. Hissela smiled and waved back. Then the escalator passed behind a wall and she vanished from sight.

My international teaching adventure had reached the final period of the final sentence of the final chapter. I had finished strong. And now, I was going home.

"Ladies and gentlemen," the stewardess' gentle voice announced over the P.A., "we are now beginning our final decent into Kansas City International Airport. Please have your tray tables up and put your seatbacks in their full upright positions. Thank you."

I had been in the United States for a few hours, mostly walking

248

up and down the terminals at George Bush International Airport between connecting flights. Just as they had in Florida three months ago, the cultural differences smacked me in the face as soon as I left the plane. Everything was green. Signs were written in English. Customs guards were horribly rude and impatient. There was a myriad of ethnic diversity. Yet, as familiar as it all felt, there was a lingering, undeniable difference. The hustle and bustle of the airport hadn't made me giddy as it had many times before. I was glad to be back, certainly, but it was a different sort of gladness. When I landed in Florida three months ago, it felt like coming home from the first day of first grade. Now, it felt like coming home after a long day of work. I was tired, and I couldn't help but feel that I had left something in Honduras. Not something I could touch, like a shirt or a book. This was something I had known my entire life, but now a piece of it was missing, and something else had replaced it entirely. There was a sadness in my heart—albeit a hopeful sadness.

The wheels skidded as the plane made first contact with the earth and slowed to a crawl. It was dark outside. As soon as the cabin lights flickered on, every passenger leapt to their feet and began unloading their bags from the overhead compartments. I sat quietly, looking out the window at the airport, now just a jet bridge away. Who awaited me inside? Would they would even recognize me now?

When it came my turn in line, I stood up and made my way to the front of the cabin. I could feel the air seeping in from the crack between the plane and the bridge. It was warm and humid, but not like San Pedro Sula. The elderly couple ahead of me took their time, walking hand in hand toward the exit. I paced behind them, passing only when they moved to the side, just before the airport door.

Stepping onto the solid floor, I rounded the corner and scanned the glass wall between the gate and a sea of eager onlookers. Faces were pressed against the glass in hopes of catching a glimpse of their loves ones. And there, in the midst of them, stood Mom and Dad. Mom had a huge smile plastered on her face. I walked through the door, as my parents greeted me with hugs and welcome-backs. "How was the plane ride? Are you hungry? You're so thin now!"

The questions continued as we marched to baggage claim, but were soon drowned out by the sound of chanting from down the hallway.

"U-S-A! U-S-A! U-S-A!"

The mantra grew louder as we came closer and closer to baggage claim, until finally we rounded the corner and the source was revealed. At the end of the hallway, holding homemade signs and wearing more red, white, and blue apparel than Uncle Sam on Independence Day, stood a group of familiar faces. As soon as we were in full view, their chanting dissolved into cheering.

It was a moment I had dreamed of for half a year. There I stood, in a land I knew, speaking a language I understood, surrounded by people that loved me.

Maybe that's what Heaven will be like, but on an infinitely more massive scale. Maybe on the day we arrive, everyone you and I have ever known will be waiting for us with signs and cheers. And maybe God will put his arm around you and me and say, "I know that was tough, but you're home now, and we've all been waiting for this day."

It was the warmest welcome I'd ever received. Two friends took my bags from the conveyer belt, and for a brief moment, we all stood together without saying a word. The moment said it for us.

Finally, Dad put his hands on his waist, looked at me, and said, "Well, are you ready to go home?"

I took another look at the faces around me.

"Yes," I said. "Yes I am."

PART SEVEN
rebuilding

Chapter 32

Culture Shock

Books end. It almost always happens when the story is finished and the reader is left satisfied. The trouble with real life, however, is that it keeps going. We're told that Snow White and Prince Charming lived happily ever after, but I'm not convinced. I imagine that once they got settled into their castle, they started arguing about the curtains or the correct direction of the toilet paper. Snow White probably had to see a doctor about the long-term effects of her coma, and Prince Charming might have had to sell his steed to pay for the castle mortgage. I'm sure their relationship required at least *some* counseling in helping the two reconcile Snow White's past of living with seven men simultaneously.

But we don't want to know those things. A good story ends at just the right moment, and the rest is left up to the imagination. After all, not everything past "Happily Ever After" is...well, happy.

My Great Honduran Adventure ended on June 19, 2014. I arrived in Kansas City to great fanfare and went to bed that night with a full heart. I was exactly where I wanted to be; I was home. My story had finally come to an end, and it was the best ending I could have dreamed of.

But when I woke up in Kansas City on June 20, I realized that I was beginning a new story, and this time, I had no idea how it would end.

The first struggle in my newfound American life was using a cell phone. Having spent six months without one, I found it such a nuisance. It weighed my shorts down, and it took so much time to type out a text message. *How did I ever live with this thing?!* I found myself thinking.

As if using a phone wasn't enough, I found driving to be terribly annoying as well. *Why can't I just walk to where I'm going?* The Midwest wasn't built for walking, and what a shame. I missed my daily cardio, and besides, driving just seemed like such a lazy way of getting around.

I had developed a routine in Honduras. It involved a lot of

reading and writing. I had no idea how vital it had become to my life until I went three days at home without it. By the end, I was exhausted—physically, mentally, emotionally, even spiritually. For the first time in my extroverted life, I *needed* alone time. It confused me, and my friends took notice. I had spent months desperately longing for community, but I quickly became irritable when I went too long without time to myself. I took a lot of long walks, usually wondering why I felt so lonely in a country where I had so many friends.

The most difficult part about being back, though, was the monotony of it all. Having no particular direction in my life, I went straight back to my old fast food job at the mall—the same one that Taylor still worked at. I clocked in that first day and stood behind the register, looking out over a busy food court. Teenagers held their phones at arm's length to snap selfies; young mothers compared new outfits with their peers; retail employees stared mindlessly into the distance, counting down the remaining minutes of their break. Had I really been climbing mountains in Central America only a week earlier? It felt like a dream. I had been thrown headlong into a culture perfectly alien from the one I'd spent half a year adjusting to. It was January all over again. But this time, I was expected to fit in.

I hadn't learned to live in Honduras; I'd learned to *survive*. Having grown up in the United States, I'd developed expectations. I knew the social norms of my own culture. When I moved to Honduras, those norms were shattered and slowly replaced with new expectations. By June, my entire perception of "normal" had evolved into something completely different. Now, being back in the U.S., I was experiencing culture shock all over again.

It occurred to me one evening that I could leave my home, drive to a restaurant, order exactly what I wanted, and go to bed on a full stomach. I actually struggled at first with whether or not I *should* do it. When I eventually gave in, I felt a sense of guilt. *Should I be leaving the house this late? Is it ok to spend this much money on food? Will they be able to understand my English?* These were issues that I wrestled with every day for months to follow.

Wal-Mart was a palace in its own right. Walking through the aisles, I couldn't help but think, *This store alone could provide for the needs of every person in Oranado for a year*. On one such occasion, a little girl ran up and tugged at my shirt. I looked down and met her big, brown eyes as she excitedly told me, "Hey! There's dog food on the floor over there, but I didn't put it there, ok?" It was beyond cute, and I couldn't help but smile and answer, "Ok, thanks for letting me know." Her mother was quick to call her back and tell me, "Sorry about that. She knows no strangers."

A wave of pride washed over me, and I basked in the joy of it. I felt accomplished, like I had just conquered the world. *I understood her! She understood me! What a success!* But after only a moment, I realized that the entire affair had happened in English. The pride I felt at such an intelligible public conversation was nothing more than my mind's struggle to properly use its newly developed language skills. It was a mental reward reserved for something else entirely.

The only thing that remained consistent from one country to the next was God. In the midst of all the chaos, my unstable sense of faith never dramatically shifted to one side or the other. God was faithful, but silent; loving, but unseen; he took me by the hand, but never squeezed tightly enough to force me into belief. I prayed, I listened, I cried, I cursed, I sang songs, I asked questions. But try as I might, I never found the assurance of my old faith. It was gone.

Maybe that's what God wanted all along. Or maybe the universe really is a cold, dark place where atoms collide randomly, and everything is meaningless. I couldn't possibly say. But my search for God, while often fruitless, never seemed to be in vain. Something—*someone*—was there, sitting in the tension with me, even if I couldn't be certain what or who.

One day, as I sat in the corner of a coffee shop with my Bible and computer, a *ding!* shot through my headphones. I looked up and saw the last thing I expected to see:
New message from Sofía Herrera.

2:31 p.m. Hello, Mark.

A smile spread across my face as I began to type.

(Mark) 2:32 p.m.   Well, hello there!

(Sofía) 2:32 p.m.   I am very sorry that I did not come to Copán that day.

(Mark) 2:33 p.m.   It's ok, Sofía.

(Sofía) 2:33 p.m.   I fell very sick. My mother had to take me to the hospital.

(Mark) 2:33 p.m.   Oh my word! Are you ok??

(Sofía) 2:34 p.m.   Yes. She takes very good care of me.

It was such a sweet relief to hear from Sofía, to know why I never got the chance to say goodbye. I knew she'd never intentionally hurt me, but that hadn't made it any easier.

(Mark) 2:36 p.m.   Sofía, I miss you.

(Sofía) 2:36 p.m.   I miss you too, Mark.

(Mark) 2:37 p.m.   How is life in Honduras? Tell me everything.

Sofía filled me in on everything over the past few months.

The students of Santa Lucia were doing well, and it looked like next year the school would host even more students. Hissela hoped to see a class all the way through to graduation (10th grade in Honduras), and then retire, knowing that her school would be self-sustaining.

Enrique was still learning new languages and climbing mountains that were never meant to be climbed.

Victoria was growing fast, and was far cuter than she had any right to be.

(Mark) 2:46 p.m.   And what about you? How are you doing?

(Sofía) 2:46 p.m.   I am well.

(Mark) 2:47 p.m.   Are you still reading your Bible?

(Sofía) 2:47 p.m.   Yes. I am trying.

(Mark) 2:47 p.m.   Good :)

For a few minutes, no other messages were sent. Sofía was almost certainly using what splotchy Wi-Fi she could find in town. There was no telling when I'd have a chance to talk with her again. This conversation was important. I'd better take full advantage.

(Mark) 2:50 p.m.   I'm praying for you, Sofía.

A moment passed. The grey bubble appeared and disappeared.

(Sofía) 2:51 p.m.   Thank you, Mark. I will not forget you.

(Mark) 2:51 p.m.   I won't forget you.

Another moment passed. Finally:

(Mark) 2:53 p.m.   Adios, amiga :)

(Sofía) 2:53 p.m.   Adios, amigo :)

Epilogue

Time. It keeps moving forward, leaving us no alternative but to come along for the ride. With each passing day, I reacclimated to North American culture, slowly, *slowly* inching out of my funk. Those closest to me did their best to understand. Still, I never quite found the words to express *why* readjusting was so difficult. I gave them little reason to love me; I guess they just *chose* to. I'll always be grateful for that.

Early that August, I re-enrolled in college, declaring Spanish as my major, and finally graduated in 2016—ten years after finishing high school.

When Christmas rolled around, a friend set me up on a blind date in Kansas City. I had always written off "love at first site" as romantic nonsense. I made the trip anyway, hoping for a fun time with a pretty girl, and nothing more.

What can I say? I was smitten from the first moment I laid eyes on her. Fifteen months later, I married that girl.

We spent a couple years in Kansas City and then moved back down to Joplin, where, once again, I re-enrolled in college and began working toward becoming a licensed teacher. The final goal is professional ESL (English as a Second Language). Come find me in a few years and I'll let you know how it's going.

I've carried these stories with me for more than three years now. They've shaped the man I am today—for better or worse. Maybe that was the plan all along, although I couldn't possibly begin to speak for God.

I wish—*oh how I wish*—that I could have written a book about the assurance of faith. Had this been a work of fiction rather than experience, I almost certainly would have encountered the risen Christ in a flash of blinding light. "Mark," he would say, "Why do you doubt? Am I not enough? Are my love and presence not tangible for your weak faith? Turn from your doubt and believe."

261

That is *not* what happened, though.

Not even close.

In fact, I'm at a loss to recall anything of the sort over the course of my entire life (with the possible exception of a few emotionally-charged worship concerts).

Maybe that does make my faith weak. Maybe I'm just not focused enough. Maybe it's a lack of discipline or an overabundance of cynicism. Maybe I just don't have the gift of faith. Or maybe I'm here to show others like me that it's ok not to know.

The bottom line is, I *don't* know.

And that's where this story ends: in the tension between belief and doubt—a place I loathe, but one from which I cannot possibly escape. If I've learned anything about this God revealed in Jesus, though, it's that he's in here with me. He knows the truth; *of course* he does. But while others belittle, rebuke, and admonish my faith, he softly whispers, "It's ok. Just focus on my voice. I know it's hard. I know. But we're gonna get through this together. Try to trust me."

It's not easy. But I'm learning to.

Author's Note

Dear Reader,

The events of this story are true. However, for the sake of those involved (people, places, and institutions), I've changed most of the names. You won't find Oranado on a map, nor will you find Santa Lucia Bilingual School on Google, because they don't exist. That's not to say the places aren't real, but I've changed the details to protect their privacy.

Any direct Scripture references are taken from the English Standard Version (ESV). It's not my favorite translation of the Bible; that honor goes to the New Living Translation (NLT). However, the Bible I used in Honduras was an ESV, and I wanted to honor the impact it had on me by writing the words exactly the way I read them during those months.

The issue of race is one that I would have rather avoided, had it not been necessary to the story. My skin is white. It's just a fact—one that I'm not particularly proud or ashamed of. It makes very little difference in the stories I tell about myself. My time in Honduras gave me my first real taste of being a minority. That's not to say it made me uncomfortable (although there were a few times when that was the case), but that I was constantly reminded of it.

The term *gringo* is a common one in Central America, and refers not only to white-skinned people, but people from the U.S. at large. Generally, it's not derogatory. As such, it felt natural to use in this book. Although it may occasionally be used offensively in the United States, this is not the case in Honduras, and should not be taken as such in the pages of this book.

One final piece of cleanup: It would make for a better story to let you believe that José made it to Maryland safely and is, as we speak, working hard to save up for his family. However, it's not true, and it would be unfair of me to let you think so. José and his band of travelers were caught at the border of Texas and temporarily put behind bars.

They were released soon after and deported back to Honduras. He has since fathered another beautiful daughter, and is working hard to provide for his family.

I wish I could tell you that I see God's hand in all of this. Again, though, that would be unfair. I don't. José was certain that his plan would succeed. He prayed and fasted for months. He sold property, including his motorcycle, to pay for the trip. But in the end, his plan failed. My conservative friends will likely say that it was God's will, carried out by the laws of the land, while my liberal friends will almost certainly say that the law is an injustice, standing in the way of God's will. I don't know which, if either is correct. All I can conclude is that bad things happen, and sometimes, all we have is the hope that one day Jesus is going to make things right. For now, I guess we're left to live in the tension and the hope that God is good, even when it's impossible to see.

From one pilgrim to another,

Mark Garnett

Acknowledgements

This book was the product of a dream, over two years in the making. I love to write, and although I have a long way to go in the learning process, the pleasure I got out of putting this story to words has been incredible.

I couldn't have done it without the advice, encouragement, and example of my friend, Whitney Cummings. I consulted her a myriad of times during the writing of this book. She is the only person I know that could find time to write and publish a book while raising two children and investing in a church, a husband, and a community. I admire you, Whitney. You're a big part of the reason this book exists today. I'm sorry I scoffed when you said I'd have to read my book at least 60-70 times during the editing process. I was wrong—so, so wrong.

I found El through a friend of a friend of a friend. She offered to edit my first chapter for free and leave it to me to decide whether to use her editing services for the remainder of the book. Hiring El was the smartest decision I made in my entire two years working on this book. El, I've said it a million times, but I'll say it again: you are amazing. Thank you for the time you invested in this book and in me.

Thanks to all those who read various drafts of the book and offered their feedback. I want to specifically thank Kirk; the ending wouldn't have been nearly as honest or meaningful without your advice.

Selah and Hugo double checked all of the Spanish in this book and helped make it sound more natural, which I am very grateful for, *porque en realidad mi español no es muy bueno...todavía*.

Mark N., I haven't known you long, man, but you've been an artistic mentor in my greatest time of need. Thanks for all the encouragement, wisdom, and energy you've given me. I don't know that I would've been able to make it these last few months without you.

I would be remiss if I didn't mention my beautiful wife, Kathleen, who also played the role of my girlfriend and fiancée during the writing of this book. She's always supported my writing, constantly encouraging me to finish this project. She created the title font from scratch and helped me arrange the original document into book format. I'd love to tell you more of our story. Maybe there's another book waiting to be written.

It would only serve to slow down the story if I mentioned every person who helped me through the lonely days in Honduras but I simply can't thank the following people enough: Tyler, Murphy, Kayla, Kelsey, Blake, Jordan, Kelsee, Alex, Selah, Shelby, Kara, Lijah, Rick, Josh, Tasha, Kathi, Sims, Quade, Jacqui, Biaka, Andrew, David, Shelly, Aaron, Erin, Aspen, and Ethan. You guys did more than you'll ever know.

Thanks to Cym and the folks at Country Meadows Baptist Church for raising the money to buy and send the books to Honduras. Thanks to Kelsey, who sent me all kinds of novels to keep me occupied, medicine to keep me alive, and candy to keep my students happy. Thanks to Mom and Dad for buying my plane ticket to Florida on such short notice and for supporting me throughout all the insanity that my trip threw at me.

My dear friend, Jordan Murdock-Thompson, is responsible for the cover art and the map. J-Murder, you're a boss. I've got this idea for a sci-fi story where the one constant throughout the multiverse is your marriage to Peter. When I finally write it, you can do the cover art.

And finally, thank you for giving this book a chance. Yes, you. Hundreds upon hundreds (probably thousands—I dunno) of hours spent working on this book would have meant nothing if you hadn't picked it up and read it. So thanks.

Copán Ruinas is a real town in western Honduras that perfectly encapsulates authentic Central American life while offering tourists loads of fun opportunities. If you enjoyed this book, I recommend you look into it. I think you'll be glad you did.

Now close this book and go explore the world.

Spanish Pronunciations

I realize how frustrating it can be to read a book with so many hard-to-pronounce words (trust me, I've read Tolkien). Out of respect for the Spanish language and those who speak it, I decided to place spelling above pronunciation in this book—although once you learn the alphabet in Spanish, you can pronounce just about any word you see.

I've provided a short index to aid those who might come across a word or two and would otherwise skip right over it. Don't worry, friends. We all have to start somewhere.

NOTE: Rather than using IPA (International Phonetic Alphabet), I did my best to spell the following words phonetically using the Latin Alphabet. If these sorts of linguistic antics make you want to pull your hair out, might I suggest you simply learn Spanish.

269

comida china	koe-MEE-dah	como estás	KOE-moe-ace-TAHS
cómo se dice	KOE-moe-sae-DEE-say	cómo te	KOE-moe-tae-
Copán Ruinas	koe-PAHN-roo-EEN-ahs	llamas	YAH-mahs
		cuántos	KWAHN-tose
cuarenta	koo-wah-RANE-tah	de	dae
de nada	dae-NAH-dah	denegado	dae-nae-GAH-doe
dengue	DANE-gae	descenso	dae-SANE-soe
días	DEE-ahs	Dios	DEE-ose
disculpe	dis-COOL-pae	Don Julio	done-HOO-lee-oe
el salto	ale-SAHL-toe	empezando	ame-pae-SAHN-doe
encantado	ane-cone-TAH-doe	Enrique	ane-REE-kae
entiendes	ane-tee-ANE-dase	entrada	ane-TRAH-dah
español	ace-pahn-YOLE	estación	ace-tah-see-YONE
estamos	ace-TAHM-ose	estúpidos	ace-TOO-pee-dose
Evi	AVE-ee	excelente	ake-sahl-ANE-tae
fantástico	fahn-TAHS-tee-coe	fe	FAE
final	fee-NAHL	frontera	frone-TAE-rah
gracias	GRAH-see-ahs	hablas	AHB-lahs
hablo	AHB-loe	hacia	ah-SEE-yah
Hissela	ee-SAE-lah	hola	OE-lah
Honduras	one-DOO-rahs	hora	OE-rah
hoy	oi	inglés	een-GLASE
Jorge	HORE-hae	José	hoe-SAE
Josué	hoe-SWAY	La Jigua	lah-HEE-goo-ah
lea	LAY-ah	lempira	lame-PEE-rah
Luis	loo-EES	Marlon	mahr-LONE
más	MAHS	Mateo	mah-TAE-oe
me llamo	mae-YAH-moe	me saludas	mae-sah-LOO-dahs
mercado	mare-CAH-doe	mucho gusto	MOO-choe-GOO-stoe
musica	MOO-see-cah	noventa	noe-VANE-tah
novia	NOE-vee-ah	pendejo	pane-DAE-hoe
perdón	pare-DONE	plancha	PLAHN-chah
platano	PLAHT-ah-noe	pobrecito	poe-brae-SEE-toe
pollo	POE-yoe	por favor	pore-fah-VOHR
por supuesto	por-soo-poo-ACE-toe	prometida	proe-mah-TEE-dah
provecho	proe-VAE-choe	Psalmos	SAHL-mose

pulperia	pool-pare-EE-yah	**qué**	KAE
quetzal	KATE-sahl	**quieres**	kee-AEY-rase
repita	rae-PEE-tah	**res**	RASE
Roatán	roe-ah-TAHN	**saluda**	sah-LOO-dah
San Pedro Sula	sahn-PADE-roe-SOO-lah	**Santa Lucia**	sahn-tah loo-SEE-ah
Santiago	sahn-tee-AH-goe	**Sarbia**	SAHR-bee-uh
señoras	sane-YOE-rahs	**señores**	sane-YOE-rase
sí	SEE	**sígueme**	SEE-gae-mae
Sofía	soe-FEE-ah	**sopa**	SOE-pah
tamale	tahm-AH-lae	**terraza**	tae-RRAH-sah
tienen	tee-ANE-ane	**tierra**	tee-AEY-rah
trabajo	trah-BAH-hoe	**turismo**	too-REES-moe
vámanos	BAHM-ahn-ose	**ven**	BANE
venir	bae-NEER	**y**	ee

For *literally* all of your writing endeavors (books, essays, short stories, papers for school, resumes, letters to the President, anonymous love letters, etc.), I cannot recommend Honeybadger Editing services highly enough. Professional work at a personal level with affordable prices.

Facebook - editingbadger
Twitter - @editingbadger
Gmail – editingbadger@gmail.com

P.O. Box 17750
Kansas City, MO 64134